APPETIZERS

150 DELICIOUS RECIPES SHOWN IN 220 STUNNING PHOTOGRAPHS

CHRISTINE INGRAM

southwater

This edition is published by Southwater,
an imprint of Anness Publishing Ltd, Blaby Road,
Wigston, Leicestershire LE18 4SE; info@anness.com

www.southwaterbooks.com; www.annesspublishing.com

If you like the images in this book and would like to
investigate using them for publishing, promotions or
advertising, please visit www.practicalpictures.com
for more information.

A CIP catalogue record for this book is available from
the British Library.

Publisher: Joanna Lorenz
Senior Managing Editor: Conor Kilgallon
Recipes: Catherine Atkinson, Alex Barker, Angela Boggiano,
Carla Capalbo, Kit Chan, Jacqueline Clarke, Maxine Clarke,
Andi Cleveley, Roz Denny, Joanna Farrow, Rafi Fernandez,
Silvano Franco, Christine France, Sarah Gates, Shirley Gill,
Nicola Graimes, Rosamund Grant, Carole Handslip,
Deh-Ta Hsiung, Peter Jordan, Elisabeth Lambert Ortiz,
Ruby Le Bois, Clare Lewis, Sara Lewis, Sally Mansfield,
Sue Maggs, Sallie Morris, Jenny Stacey, Hilaire Walden,
Laura Washburn, Steven Wheeler, Kate Whiteman,
Elizabeth Wolf-Cohen and Jenni Wright
Photography: Karl Adamson, Edward Allwright,
Steve Baxter, James Duncan, John Freeman, Ian Garlick,
Michelle Garrett, Peter Henley, John Heseltine, Janine
Hosegood, Amanda Heywood, David Jordan, Maria Kelly,
Dave King, Don Last, William Lingwood, Patrick McLeavey,
Michael Michaels, Thomas Odulate and Sam Stowell
Designed and Edited for Anness Publishing Ltd by
the Bridgewater Book Company Ltd
Production Controller: Wendy Lawson

NOTES

Bracketed terms are intended for American readers.
For all recipes, quantities are given in both metric and
imperial measures and, where appropriate, in standard
cups and spoons. Follow one set of measures, but not
a mixture, because they are not interchangeable.
Standard spoon and cup measures are level. 1 tsp = 5ml,
1 tbsp = 15ml, 1 cup = 250ml/8fl oz.
Australian standard tablespoons are 20ml. Australian
readers should use 3 tsp in place of 1 tbsp for measuring
small quantities.
American pints are 16fl oz/2 cups. American readers
should use 20fl oz/2.5 cups in place of 1 pint when
measuring liquids.
Electric oven temperatures in this book are for
conventional ovens. When using a fan oven, the
temperature will probably need to be reduced by about
10–20°C/20–40°F. Since ovens vary, you should check
with your manufacturer's instruction book for guidance.
The nutritional analysis given for each recipe is calculated
per portion (i.e. serving or item), unless otherwise stated.
If the recipe gives a range, such as Serves 4–6, then the
nutritional analysis will be for the smaller portion size,
i.e. 6 servings. The analysis does not include optional
ingredients, such as salt added to taste.
Medium (US large) eggs are used unless otherwise stated.
Front cover shows Parmesan fish goujons – for recipe,
see page 27.

APPETIZERS

Contents

Introduction   6

DIPS AND NIBBLES   **8**

SOUPS, PÂTÉS AND TERRINES   **50**

VEGETARIAN DISHES   **98**

FISH AND SHELLFISH   **134**

POULTRY AND MEAT   **172**

SALADS   **194**

Guide to techniques   216

Index   222

Introduction

Appetizers can be the best part of a meal and many people prefer them to larger courses. Indeed, they are so popular that sometimes whole dinner parties consist entirely of a variety of appetizers. You can see the attraction – "starters" by definition indicate small portions, which means there can be a huge and delicious selection of different and interesting dishes. Of course, for the cook, having to provide such a medley of diverse foods can be quite a challenge (although one you may well feel equal to), but for the guests it will be nothing less than a complete delight!

In some countries, appetizers or "starters" have become an institution. Tapas, in Spain, are a meal in their own right, and the Italians' antipasto is so varied and delicious that you'd be forgiven for wishing to stop right there with the artichokes and superb dried hams, and forget entirely about the pasta and meat that follow.

If you're planning a sophisticated dinner party, it is possible to start with a simple but tasty appetizer such as Pork and Peanut Wontons with Plum Sauce or Leek and Onion Tartlets, which can be served easily beforehand with drinks. Your choice of appetizer should take its cue from the food you intend to serve

as a main course. Choose this with care, as the appetizer will set the tone for the rest of the meal. Select something fairly light, such as grilled king prawns (jumbo shrimp) or a simple salad if you

BELOW *Serve Potted Prawns with crunchy brown toast or crackers.*

ABOVE: *A very tasty starter can be easily made from a few simple ingredients.*

ABOVE: *A terrine makes a colourful addition to any menu.*

ABOVE: *Salads make great starters, as they are quick and simple to prepare.*

plan to serve a roast meat or hearty stew. If, on the other hand, you are barbecuing fish or grilling chicken, you could decide on something much more elaborate such as Wild Mushroom and Fontina Tarts, or fish or vegetable terrines, which look pretty and taste wonderful. Or, for an Oriental meal, you could serve Chicken Satay with Peanut Sauce.

However, you shouldn't feel too constrained by the ethnicity of your meal. Today, the trend is to serve foods that complement each other. A Mediterranean-style starter such as Charred Artichokes with Lemon Oil Dip could happily come before an Indonesian green curry. Similarly,

Malayan Prawn Laksa would be fine before a French or Italian-style meal.

Those rules that do exist are related to texture and taste. For example, if you're making a soufflé or roulade as a main course, choose something crunchy as a starter.

The recipes in this book are extremely versatile and can be used for a range of occasions such as a buffet party, a light lunch, as finger food for an informal dinner party or as pre-dinner nibbles. And the beauty of many of the dishes is that they are incredibly simple and quick to make and can look stunning with very little effort – they will get any meal off to the best possible start.

USING THIS BOOK

This book is ideal for first-time cooks with a passion for appetizers, who will benefit from the detailed Guide to Techniques section at the end of the book as well as the more straightforward Dips and Nibbles section at the front. It will also appeal to the more experienced cook, who will find elaborate dishes in the Soups, Pâtés and Terrines section, as well as more difficult recipes to tackle in the Fish and Shellfish and Poultry and Meat sections.

Dips and nibbles

The recipes in this section are perfect for many occasions. Treats such as Parmesan Thins and Duck Wontons with Spicy Mango Sauce can be served as part of a buffet or as finger food at a drinks party. Dips lend piquancy and interest to finger food. Potato Skins with Cajun Dip make an unusual and exciting starter or try hot crispy Celeriac Fritters with cold Mustard Dip for an exciting flavour combination.

Hummus bi tahina

Blending chickpeas with garlic and oil creates a surprisingly creamy purée that is delicious as part of a Turkish-style mezze, or as a dip with vegetables. Leftovers make a good sandwich filler.

SERVES 4–6

150g/5oz/3/4 cup dried chickpeas
juice of 2 lemons
2 garlic cloves, sliced
30ml/2 tbsp olive oil
pinch of cayenne pepper

150ml/1/4 pint/2/3 cup tahini paste
salt and ground black pepper
extra olive oil and cayenne pepper,
     for sprinkling
flat leaf parsley sprigs, to garnish

1 Put the chickpeas in a bowl with plenty of cold water and leave them to soak overnight.

2 Drain the chickpeas, place in a pan and cover with fresh water. Bring to the boil and boil rapidly for 10 minutes. Reduce the heat and simmer gently for about 1 hour until soft. Drain in a colander.

3 Process the chickpeas in a food processor to a smooth purée. Add the lemon juice, garlic, olive oil, cayenne pepper and tahini paste and blend until creamy, scraping the mixture down from the sides of the bowl.

4 Season the purée with plenty of salt and ground black pepper and transfer to a serving dish. Sprinkle with a little olive oil and cayenne pepper, and serve garnished with a few parsley sprigs.

COOK'S TIP
For convenience, canned chickpeas can be used instead. Allow two 400g/14oz cans and drain them thoroughly. Tahini paste can now be purchased from most good supermarkets or health food shops.

Nutritional information per portion: Energy 265kcal/1101kJ; Protein 10g; Carbohydrate 12.6g, of which sugars 0.8g; Fat 19.7g, of which saturates 2.8g; Cholesterol 0mg; Calcium 210mg; Fibre 4.7g; Sodium 15mg.

Potato skins with Cajun dip

Divinely crisp and naughty, these potato skins are really simple to make. They are great on their own or served with this piquant dip as a garnish or on the side.

SERVES 4

2 large baking potatoes
vegetable oil, for deep-frying

FOR THE DIP

120ml/4fl oz/¹/₂ cup natural
    (plain) yogurt
1 garlic clove, crushed
5ml/1 tsp tomato purée (paste) or
    2.5ml/¹/₂ tsp green chilli purée or
    ¹/₂ small green chilli, chopped
1.5ml/¹/₄ tsp celery salt
salt and ground black pepper

1 Preheat the oven to 180°C/350°F/Gas 4. Bake the potatoes for 45–50 minutes until they are tender.

2 Cut the potatoes in half and then scoop out the flesh, leaving a thin layer on the skins. Keep the flesh for another meal. Cut the potatoes in half once more.

3 To make the dip, mix together all the ingredients and chill.

4 Heat a 1cm/¹/₂in layer of oil in a pan or deep-fryer. Fry the potatoes until they are crisp and golden. Drain on kitchen paper, then sprinkle with salt and black pepper. Serve the potato skins with a bowl of dip or a dollop of dip in each skin.

Nutritional information per portion: Energy 210kcal/871kJ; Protein 2.7g; Carbohydrate 12.5g, of which sugars 3.3g; Fat 17g, of which saturates 2.2g; Cholesterol 0mg; Calcium 61mg; Fibre 0.7g; Sodium 35mg.

Celeriac fritters with mustard dip

Celeriac is an unusual vegetable with a deliciously subtle flavour. Here it is used to make hot, crispy fritters which taste fabulous combined with a cold mustard dip.

SERVES 4

1 egg
115g/4oz/1½ cups ground almonds
45ml/3 tbsp freshly grated
   Parmesan cheese
45ml/3 tbsp chopped fresh parsley
1 celeriac, about 450g/1lb
lemon juice
oil, for deep-frying
salt and ground black pepper
sea salt flakes, to garnish

FOR THE DIP
150ml/¼ pint/⅔ cup sour cream
15–30ml/1–2 tbsp wholegrain mustard

1 Beat the egg well and pour into a shallow dish. Mix together the almonds, Parmesan and parsley in a separate dish. Season well.

2 Peel and cut the celeriac into batons about 1cm/½in wide and 5cm/2in long. Drop them into a bowl of water with a little lemon juice added to prevent discoloration.

3 Heat the oil to 180°C/350°F. Drain and then pat dry half the celeriac batons. Dip them into the beaten egg, then into the ground almond mixture, coating the pieces completely and evenly.

4 Deep-fry the fritters, in batches, for 2–3 minutes until golden. Drain on kitchen paper. Keep warm while you cook the remaining fritters.

5 Mix the dip ingredients together with salt to taste. Spoon into a bowl. Sprinkle the fritters with sea salt flakes.

Nutritional information per portion: Energy 514kcal/2123kJ; Protein 14.3g; Carbohydrate 4.7g, of which sugars 4g; Fat 48.8g, of which saturates 11g; Cholesterol 81mg; Calcium 301mg; Fibre 3.7g; Sodium 349mg.

Basil and lemon dip

This lovely dip is based on fresh mayonnaise flavoured with lemon juice and two types of basil, green and opal. Serve with crispy potato wedges for a delicious starter.

SERVES 4

2 large egg yolks
15ml/1 tbsp lemon juice
150ml/¼ pint/²⁄₃ cup olive oil
150ml/¼ pint/²⁄₃ cup sunflower oil

4 garlic cloves
handful of fresh green basil
handful of fresh opal basil
salt and ground black pepper

1 Place the egg yolks and lemon juice into a blender or food processor and process them briefly until they are lightly blended.

2 In a jug (pitcher), stir together the oils. With the machine running, pour in the oil very slowly, a little at a time. Once half of the oil has been added, the remaining oil can be incorporated more quickly. Continue processing to form a thick, creamy mayonnaise.

3 Peel and crush the garlic cloves. Alternatively, place them on a chopping board and sprinkle with salt, then flatten them with the heel of a heavy-bladed knife and chop the flesh. Flatten the garlic again to make a coarse purée.

4 Tear both types of basil into small pieces and then stir into the mayonnaise along with the crushed garlic.

5 Add salt and pepper to taste, then transfer the dip to a serving dish. Cover and chill until ready to serve.

COOK'S TIP
Make sure all the ingredients are at room temperature before you start to help prevent the mixture from curdling.

Nutritional information per portion: Energy 210kcal/871kJ; Protein 2.7g; Carbohydrate 12.5g, of which sugars 3.3g; Fat 17g, of which saturates 2.2g; Cholesterol 0mg; Calcium 61mg; Fibre 0.7g; Sodium 35mg.

Guacamole

Avocados discolour quickly, so make this sauce just before serving. If you do need to keep it for any length of time, cover the surface of the sauce with clear film and chill in the fridge.

SERVES 6

2 large ripe avocados
2 red chillies, seeded
1 garlic clove
1 shallot
20ml/2 tbsp olive oil, plus extra to serve
juice of 1 lemon
salt and ground black pepper
flat leaf parsley leaves, to garnish

1 Halve the avocados, remove the stones and scoop out the flesh into a large bowl.

2 Using a fork or potato masher, mash the avocado until smooth.

3 Finely chop the chillies, garlic and shallot, then stir into the mashed avocado with the olive oil and lemon juice. Season to taste with salt and ground black pepper.

4 Spoon the mixture into a small serving bowl. Drizzle over a little olive oil and scatter with a few flat leaf parsley leaves. Serve straight away.

Nutritional information per portion: Energy 108kcal/445kJ; Protein 1.6g; Carbohydrate 3.1g, of which sugars 2.3g; Fat 9.9g, of which saturates 2.1g; Cholesterol 0mg; Calcium 13mg; Fibre 2.3g; Sodium 8mg.

Thai tempeh cakes with dipping sauce

Made from soya beans, tempeh is similar to tofu but has a nuttier taste. Here, it is combined with a fragrant blend of lemon grass, coriander and ginger, and formed into small patties.

MAKES 8 CAKES

1 lemon grass stalk, finely chopped
2 each garlic cloves, spring onions
  (scallions) and shallots, finely chopped
2 chillies, seeded and finely chopped
2.5cm/1 in piece fresh root ginger, chopped
60ml/4 tbsp chopped fresh coriander
  (cilantro), plus extra to garnish
250g/9oz/2¼ cups tempeh, sliced
15ml/1 tbsp lime juice
5ml/1 tsp caster (superfine) sugar
45ml/3 tbsp plain (all-purpose) flour
1 large egg, lightly beaten
vegetable oil, for frying
salt and freshly ground black pepper

FOR THE DIPPING SAUCE

45ml/3 tbsp each mirin (sweet rice wine)
  and wine vinegar
2 spring onions (scallions), finely sliced
15ml/1 tbsp sugar
2 chillies, finely chopped
30ml/2 tbsp chopped fresh coriander
  (cilantro)

1 To make the dipping sauce, mix together the mirin, vinegar, spring onions, sugar, chillies and coriander in a small bowl and set aside.

2 Place the lemon grass, garlic, spring onions, shallots, chillies, ginger and coriander in a food processor or blender. Process to a coarse paste. Add the tempeh, lime juice and sugar, then blend until combined. Add the flour and egg, and season. Process again until the mixture forms a coarse, sticky paste.

3 Take a heaped serving-spoonful of the paste mixture at a time and form into rounds with your hands. The mixture at this stage will be quite sticky.

4 Heat enough oil to cover the base of a large frying pan. Fry the tempeh cakes for 5–6 minutes, turning once, until they are golden on both sides. Drain on kitchen paper and serve warm with the dipping sauce, garnished with the extra chopped fresh coriander.

Nutritional information per portion: Energy 79kcal/332kJ; Protein 4.5g; Carbohydrate 9.1g, of which sugars 4.3g; Fat 2.3g, of which saturates 0.4g; Cholesterol 26mg; Calcium 192mg; Fibre 0.8g; Sodium 15mg.

Lemon and coconut dhal

A warm spicy dish with tangy lemon and coconut flavours, this can be served either as a dip with warmed pitta bread or as an accompaniment to cold meats.

SERVES 8

5cm/2in piece fresh root ginger
1 onion
2 garlic cloves
2 small red chillies, seeded
30ml/2 tbsp sunflower oil
5ml/1 tsp cumin seeds, plus extra
    to garnish

150g/5oz/²⁄₃ cup red lentils
250ml/8fl oz/1 cup water
15ml/1 tbsp hot curry paste
200ml/7fl oz/scant 1 cup coconut cream
juice of 1 lemon
25g/1oz/¹⁄₄ cup flaked (sliced) almonds
salt and ground black pepper

1 Use a vegetable peeler to peel the ginger and finely chop it with the onion, garlic and chillies.

2 Heat the sunflower oil in a large, shallow pan. Add the ginger, onion, garlic, chillies and cumin. Cook for about 5 minutes, until the onion is softened but not coloured.

3 Stir the lentils, water and curry paste into the pan. Bring to the boil, cover and cook gently over a low heat for about 15–20 minutes, stirring occasionally, until the lentils are just tender and not yet broken up.

4 Stir in all but 30ml/2 tbsp of the coconut cream. Bring to the boil and cook, uncovered, for a further 15–20 minutes, until the mixture is thick and pulpy. Off the heat, stir in the lemon juice. Season to taste.

5 Heat a large frying pan and cook the flaked almonds for one or two minutes on each side until golden brown. Stir about three-quarters of the toasted almonds into the dhal.

6 Transfer the dhal to a serving bowl; swirl in the remaining coconut cream. Scatter the reserved almonds on top with the cumin seeds and serve warm.

Nutritional information per portion: Energy 190kcal/791kJ; Protein 6g; Carbohydrate 12.2g, of which sugars 1.9g; Fat 13.4g, of which saturates 7.9g; Cholesterol 0mg; Calcium 22mg; Fibre 1.3g; Sodium 11mg.

Baba ganoush with Lebanese flatbread

Baba ganoush is a delectable aubergine dip which comes from the Middle East. Tahini – a sesame seed paste with cumin – gives the dish a hint of spice.

SERVES 6

2 small aubergines (eggplants)
1 garlic clove, crushed
60ml/4 tbsp tahini
25g/1oz/¼ cup ground almonds
juice of ½ lemon
2.5ml/½ tsp ground cumin
30ml/2 tbsp fresh mint leaves
30ml/2 tbsp olive oil
salt and ground black pepper

FOR THE FLATBREAD

4 pitta breads
45ml/3 tbsp sesame seeds
45ml/3 tbsp fresh thyme leaves
45ml/3 tbsp poppy seeds
150ml/¼ pint/²/₃ cup olive oil

1 First make the Lebanese flatbread. Split the pitta breads through the middle and open them out. Mix the sesame seeds, chopped thyme and poppy seeds in a mortar. Crush them with a pestle to release the flavour.

2 Stir in the olive oil. Spread the mixture over the cut sides of the pitta bread. Grill (broil) until golden. When cool, break into pieces and set aside.

3 Grill (broil) the aubergines, turning them frequently, until the skin is blackened and blistered. Remove the skin, then chop the flesh roughly and leave to drain in a colander.

4 Squeeze out as much liquid from the aubergine as possible. Place the flesh in a blender or food processor, then add the garlic, tahini, ground almonds, lemon juice and cumin, with salt to taste. Process to a smooth paste, then roughly chop half the mint and stir into the dip.

5 Spoon the paste into a bowl, scatter the remaining mint leaves on top and drizzle with the olive oil. Serve with the Lebanese flatbread.

Nutritional information per portion: Energy 451kcal/1878kJ; Protein 9.3g; Carbohydrate 29.5g, of which sugars 3.1g; Fat 33.8g, of which saturates 4.7g; Cholesterol 0mg; Calcium 204mg; Fibre 4.2g; Sodium 225mg.

Quail's eggs with herbs and dips

For al fresco eating or informal entertaining, this colourful platter of contrasting tastes and textures is delicious. Choose the best seasonal vegetables available.

SERVES 6

1 large Italian focaccia or 2–3 Indian
    parathas or other flatbread
olive oil
1 large garlic clove, finely chopped
small handful of chopped fresh mixed
    herbs, such as coriander (cilantro),
    mint, parsley and oregano
18–24 quail's eggs
salt and ground black pepper

FOR THE DIPS
30ml/2 tbsp home-made mayonnaise
30ml/2 tbsp thick sour cream
5ml/1 tsp chopped capers

5ml/1 tsp finely chopped shallot
salt and ground black pepper

TO SERVE
225g/8oz fresh beetroot (beet), cooked in
    water or cider, peeled and sliced
1/2 bunch spring onions (scallions),
    trimmed and roughly chopped
60ml/4 tbsp red onion or tamarind and
    date chutney
high quality olive oil
coarse sea salt and mixed
    ground peppercorns

1 Preheat the oven to 190°C/375°F/Gas 5. Brush the focaccia or flatbread liberally with oil, sprinkle with garlic, the herbs and seasoning and bake for 10–15 minutes, or until golden. Keep warm.

2 Put the quail's eggs into a saucepan of cold water, bring to the boil and boil for 5 minutes. Arrange in a serving dish. Peel the eggs if you wish or leave guests to do their own.

3 To make the dip, combine the mayonnaise, soured cream, capers, shallot and seasoning.

4 To serve, cut the bread into wedges and serve with dishes of the quail's eggs, mayonnaise dip, sliced beetroot, chopped spring onion and chutney. Serve with tiny bowls of coarse salt and ground peppercorns, together with olive oil for dipping.

Nutritional information per portion: Energy 344kcal/1446kJ; Protein 15.7g; Carbohydrate 43.6g, of which sugars 8.3g; Fat 13.2g, of which saturates 3.4g; Cholesterol 260mg; Calcium 151mg; Fibre 2.7g; Sodium 478mg.

Chilli bean dip

This deliciously spicy and creamy bean dip is best served warm, either with triangles of lightly grilled pitta bread or a large bowl of crunchy tortilla chips.

SERVES 4

2 garlic cloves
1 onion
2 green chillies
30ml/2 tbsp vegetable oil
5–10ml/1–2 tsp hot chilli powder

400g/14oz can kidney beans
75g/3oz mature (sharp) Cheddar
   cheese, grated
1 red chilli, seeded
salt and ground black pepper

1 Finely chop the garlic and onion. Seed and finely chop the green chillies.

2 Heat the vegetable oil in a heavy pan or deep frying pan and add the garlic, onion, green chillies and chilli powder. Cook gently for about 5 minutes, stirring regularly, until the onions are softened and transparent, but not browned.

3 Drain the kidney beans, reserving the liquid. Blend all but 30ml/2 tbsp of the beans to a purée in a food processor.

4 Add the puréed beans to the pan with 30–45ml/2–3 tbsp of the reserved liquor. Heat gently, stirring to mix well.

5 Stir in the whole beans and the Cheddar cheese. Cook gently for about 2–3 minutes, stirring until the cheese melts. Add salt and pepper to taste.

6 Cut the red chilli into thin strips. Spoon the dip into four individual serving bowls and scatter the chilli strips over the top. Serve warm.

COOK'S TIP
For a dip with a coarser texture, do not purée the beans; instead mash them with a potato masher.

Nutritional information per portion: Energy 244kcal/1018kJ; Protein 12.7g; Carbohydrate 20.2g, of which sugars 4.6g; Fat 12.6g, of which saturates 4.8g; Cholesterol 18mg; Calcium 234mg; Fibre 7.1g; Sodium 538mg.

King prawns in crispy batter

Serve these delightfully crispy prawns with an Oriental-style dipping sauce or, for something a little different, offer a simple tomato sauce or lemon wedges for squeezing.

SERVES 4

120ml/4fl oz/½ cup water
1 egg
115g/4oz/1 cup plain (all-purpose) flour
5ml/1 tsp cayenne pepper
12 raw king prawns (jumbo
    shrimp), unpeeled
vegetable oil, for deep-frying
flat leaf parsley, to garnish
lemon wedges, to serve

FOR THE DIPPING SAUCE

30ml/2 tbsp soy sauce
30ml/2 tbsp dry sherry
10ml/2 tsp clear honey

1 In a bowl, whisk the water with the egg. Add the flour and cayenne, and whisk to make a smooth batter.

2 Carefully peel the prawns, leaving just the tail sections intact. Make a shallow cut down the back of each prawn, then pull out and discard the dark intestinal tract.

3 To make the dipping sauce, mix the soy sauce, dry sherry and honey in a small bowl until well combined.

4 Heat the oil in a large pan or deep-fryer, until a cube of stale bread browns in 1 minute.

5 Holding the prawns by their tails, dip them into the batter, one at a time, shaking off any excess. Drop the prawns carefully into the oil and fry for 2–3 minutes until crisp and golden brown. Drain on kitchen paper and serve with the dipping sauce and lemon wedges, garnished with parsley.

Nutritional information per portion: Energy 278kcal/1162kJ; Protein 8.9g; Carbohydrate 25g, of which sugars 3g; Fat 15.7g, of which saturates 2.1g; Cholesterol 96mg; Calcium 69mg; Fibre 0.9g; Sodium 601mg.

Parmesan fish goujons

Use this batter, with or without the cheese, whenever you feel brave enough to fry fish. This is light and crisp, just like authentic fish-and-chip shop batter.

SERVES 4

375g/13oz plaice or sole fillets, or thicker
   fish such as cod or haddock
a little plain (all-purpose) flour
oil, for deep-frying
salt and ground black pepper
dill sprigs, to garnish

FOR THE CREAM SAUCE

60ml/4 tbsp sour cream
60ml/4 tbsp mayonnaise
2.5ml/½ tsp grated lemon rind
30ml/2 tbsp chopped gherkins or capers
15ml/1 tbsp chopped mixed fresh herbs,
   or 5ml/1 tsp dried

FOR THE BATTER

75g/3oz/¾ cup plain (all purpose) flour
25g/1oz/¼ cup grated Parmesan cheese
5ml/1 tsp bicarbonate of soda (baking
   soda)
1 egg, separated
150ml/¼ pint/⅔ cup milk

1 To make the sauce, mix the cream, mayonnaise, lemon rind, gherkins or capers, herbs and seasoning together, then chill in the fridge.

2 To make the batter, sift the flour into a bowl. Mix in the other dry ingredients and some salt, and then whisk in the egg yolk and milk to give a thick yet smooth batter. Then gradually whisk in 90ml/6 tbsp water. Season and chill in the fridge.

3 Skin the fish and cut into thin strips of similar length. Dip the fish lightly in seasoned flour.

4 Heat at least 5cm/2in oil in a large, heavy pan with a lid. Whisk the egg white until stiff and gently fold into the batter until just blended.

5 Dip the floured fish into the batter, drain off any excess and then drop gently into the hot fat.

6 Cook the fish in batches, so that the goujons don't stick to one another, for only 3–4 minutes, turning once. When the batter is golden and crisp, remove the fish with a slotted spoon. Place the goujons on kitchen paper on a plate and keep warm while cooking the rest. Serve hot, garnished with sprigs of dill and accompanied by the cream sauce.

Nutritional information per portion: Energy 358kcal/1497kJ; Protein 24.2g; Carbohydrate 21.4g, of which sugars 3.2g; Fat 20.2g, of which saturates 5.9g; Cholesterol 116mg; Calcium 243mg; Fibre 1.4g; Sodium 293mg.

King prawns with spicy dip

The spicy dip served with this dish is equally good made from peanuts instead of cashew nuts. Vegetarians can enjoy this, too, if you make it with vegetables or tofu cubes.

SERVES 4–6

24 raw king prawns (jumbo
    shrimp), unpeeled
juice of ½ lemon
5ml/1 tsp paprika
1 bay leaf
1 thyme sprig
vegetable oil, for brushing
salt and ground black pepper

FOR THE SPICY DIP
1 onion, chopped
4 canned plum tomatoes, plus 60ml/
    4 tbsp of the juice
½ green (bell) pepper, seeded
    and chopped
1 garlic clove, crushed
15ml/1 tbsp cashew nuts
15ml/1 tbsp soy sauce
15ml/1 tbsp desiccated (dry
    unsweetened shredded) coconut

1 Peel the prawns, leaving the tails on. Place in a shallow dish and sprinkle with the lemon juice, paprika and seasoning. Cover and chill in the fridge.

2 Put the prawn shells in a pan with the bay leaf and thyme, cover with water, and bring to the boil. Simmer for 30 minutes; strain the stock into a measuring jug. Top up with water, if necessary, to 300ml/½ pint/1¼ cups.

3 For the dip, place the ingredients in a blender or food processor and process until smooth. Pour into a pan with the stock and simmer over a moderate heat for 30 minutes, until the sauce is fairly thick.

4 Preheat the grill (broiler). Thread the prawns on to small skewers, then brush the prawns on both sides with a little oil and grill (broil) under a low heat until cooked, turning once. Serve with the dip.

Nutritional information per portion: Energy 80kcal/334kJ; Protein 9.9g; Carbohydrate 3g, of which sugars 2.3g; Fat 3.2g, of which saturates 1.7g; Cholesterol 98mg; Calcium 46mg; Fibre 0.9g; Sodium 283mg.

Beef satay with a hot mango dip

Strips of tender beef are flavoured with a warmly spiced marinade before being cooked on skewers, then served with a tangy fruit dip.

MAKES 12 SKEWERS

450g/1lb sirloin steak, 2cm/³/4 in thick
15ml/1 tbsp coriander seeds
5ml/1 tsp cumin seeds
50g/2oz/¹/3 cup raw cashew nuts
15ml/1 tbsp vegetable oil
2 shallots or 1 small onion, finely chopped
1cm/¹/2in piece fresh root ginger
1 garlic clove, crushed
30ml/2 tbsp each tamarind and soy sauce
10ml/2 tsp sugar
5ml/1 tsp rice or white wine vinegar

FOR THE MANGO DIP

1 ripe mango
1–2 small red chillies, seeded and chopped
15ml/1 tbsp fish sauce
juice of 1 lime
10ml/2 tsp sugar
1.5ml/¹/4 tsp salt
30ml/2 tbsp fresh coriander (cilantro)

1 Soak 12 bamboo skewers for 30 minutes. Slice the beef into long narrow strips and thread, zigzag-style, on to the skewers. Lay on a flat plate and set aside.

2 For the marinade, dry-fry the seeds and nuts in a large wok until evenly brown. Transfer to a mortar with a rough surface and crush finely with the pestle. Peel and chop the ginger. Add the oil, shallots or onion, ginger, garlic, tamarind and soy sauces, sugar and vinegar.

3 Spread this marinade over the beef and leave to marinate for up to 8 hours. Cook the beef under a moderate grill (broiler) or over a barbecue for 6–8 minutes, turning to ensure an even colour. Meanwhile, make the mango dip.

4 Cut away the skin and remove the stone (pit) from the mango. Process the mango flesh with the chillies, fish sauce, lime juice, sugar and salt until smooth, then add the coriander and serve with the beef.

Nutritional information per portion: Energy 62kcal/263kJ; Protein 9g; Carbohydrate 2.9g, of which sugars 2.8g; Fat 1.7g, of which saturates 0.8g; Cholesterol 19mg; Calcium 5mg; Fibre 0.3g; Sodium 205mg.

Pork balls with a minted peanut sauce

This makes an unusual and exotic starter for a dinner party or as part of a buffet. The recipe is equally delicious made with chicken breasts.

SERVES 4–6

275g/10oz leg of pork, trimmed and diced
1cm/^{1}/$_2$in piece fresh root ginger, grated
1 garlic clove, crushed
10ml/2 tsp sesame oil
15ml/1 tbsp each sherry and soy sauce
5ml/1 tsp sugar
1 egg white
salt and white pepper, to taste
350g/12oz/scant 1^3/$_4$ cups long grain
    rice, cooked for 15 minutes
50g/2oz ham, diced
1 iceberg lettuce, to serve

FOR THE PEANUT SAUCE

15ml/1 tbsp coconut cream
75ml/2^1/$_2$fl oz/^{1}/$_3$ cup boiling water
30ml/2 tbsp smooth peanut butter
juice of 1 lime
1 red chilli, seeded and finely chopped
1 garlic clove, crushed
15ml/1 tbsp chopped fresh mint
15ml/1 tbsp chopped fresh coriander
    (cilantro)

1 Place the diced pork, ginger and garlic in a food processor, and then process for 2–3 minutes until smooth. Add the sesame oil, sherry, soy sauce and sugar and blend with the pork mixture. Finally, add the egg white, salt and white pepper.

2 Spread the cooked rice and ham in a shallow dish. Using wet hands, shape the pork mixture into thumb-size balls. Roll in the rice to coat and pierce each ball with a bamboo skewer.

3 To make the peanut sauce, put the coconut cream in a measuring jug and cover with the boiling water. Place the peanut butter in another bowl with the lime juice, chilli, garlic, mint and coriander. Combine evenly then add the coconut.

4 Place the pork balls in a bamboo steamer and steam over a saucepan of boiling water for 8–10 minutes. Arrange the pork balls on lettuce leaves on a plate, with the sauce to one side.

Nutritional information per portion: Energy 337kcal/1409kJ; Protein 17.5g; Carbohydrate 47.9g, of which sugars 1g; Fat 7.8g, of which saturates 3g; Cholesterol 33mg; Calcium 35mg; Fibre 0.7g; Sodium 322mg.

Pork and peanut wontons with plum sauce

These crispy filled wontons are delicious served with a sweet plum sauce. The wontons can be filled and set aside for up to eight hours before they are cooked.

MAKES 40–50 WONTONS

**175g/6oz/1½ cups minced (ground) pork
or 175g/6oz pork sausages, skinned
2 spring onions (scallions), finely chopped
30ml/2 tbsp peanut butter
10ml/2 tsp oyster sauce (optional)
40–50 wonton skins
30ml/2 tbsp flour paste
vegetable oil, for deep-frying
salt and ground black pepper
lettuce and radishes, to garnish**

FOR THE PLUM SAUCE

**225g/8oz/generous ¾ cup dark
plum jam
15ml/1 tbsp rice or white wine vinegar
15ml/1 tbsp dark soy sauce
2.5ml/½ tsp chilli sauce**

1 Combine the minced pork or skinned sausages, spring onions, peanut butter, oyster sauce, if using, and seasoning, and then set aside.

2 For the sauce, combine the plum jam, vinegar, soy and chilli sauces in a serving bowl and set aside.

3 To fill the wonton skins, place 8 wrappers at a time on a work surface, moisten the edges with the flour paste and place 2.5ml/½ tsp of the filling on each one. Fold in half, corner to corner, and twist.

4 Fill a wok or deep frying pan one-third with vegetable oil and heat to 190°C/375°F. Have ready a wire strainer or frying basket and a tray lined with kitchen paper. Drop the wontons, 8 at a time, into the hot fat and then fry until they are golden all over, for about 1–2 minutes. Lift out on to the paper-lined tray, using a slotted spoon and sprinkle with fine salt.

5 Serve the wontons with the plum sauce, garnished with the lettuce and radishes.

Nutritional information per portion: Energy 56kcal/236kJ; Protein 1.5g; Carbohydrate 7.9g, of which sugars 4.1g; Fat 2.3g, of which saturates 0.4g; Cholesterol 3mg; Calcium 8mg; Fibre 0.2g; Sodium 35mg.

Chicken satay with peanut sauce

These skewers of marinated chicken can be prepared in advance and served at room temperature. Beef, pork or even lamb fillet can be used instead of chicken if you prefer.

MAKES ABOUT 24

450g/1lb skinless chicken
   breast fillets
oil, for brushing
sesame seeds, for sprinkling
red pepper strips, to garnish

FOR THE MARINADE
90ml/6 tbsp vegetable oil
60ml/4 tbsp tamari or light soy sauce
60ml/4 tbsp fresh lime juice
2.5cm/1in piece fresh root ginger, peeled
   and chopped
3–4 garlic cloves
30ml/2 tbsp light brown sugar

5ml/1 tsp Chinese-style chilli sauce or
   1 red chilli, seeded and chopped
30ml/2 tbsp chopped fresh coriander
   (cilantro)

FOR THE PEANUT SAUCE
30ml/2 tbsp smooth peanut butter
30ml/2 tbsp soy sauce
15ml/1 tbsp sesame or vegetable oil
2 spring onions (scallions), chopped
2 garlic cloves
15–30ml/1–2 tbsp fresh lime or
   lemon juice
15ml/1 tbsp brown sugar

1 Prepare the marinade. Place all the marinade ingredients in a food processor or blender and process until smooth and well blended, scraping down the sides of the bowl once. Pour into a shallow dish and set aside.

2 Into the same food processor or blender, put all the peanut sauce ingredients and process until well blended. If the sauce is too thick, add a little water and process again. Pour into a bowl and cover until ready to serve.

3 Slice the chicken breast fillets into thin strips, then cut the strips into 2cm/³⁄₄in pieces. Add the chicken pieces to the marinade in the dish. Toss well to coat, cover and marinate for about 3–4 hours in a cool place, or overnight in the fridge.

4 Preheat the grill (broiler). Line a baking sheet with foil and brush lightly with oil. Thread 2–3 pieces of marinated chicken on to skewers and sprinkle with the sesame seeds. Grill (broil) for 4–5 minutes until golden, turning once. Serve with the peanut sauce, and a garnish of red pepper strips.

Nutritional information per portion: Energy 48kcal/200kJ; Protein 4.8g; Carbohydrate 2.2g, of which sugars 2.1g; Fat 2.2g, of which saturates 0.4g; Cholesterol 13mg; Calcium 3mg; Fibre 0.1g; Sodium 105mg.

Duck wontons with spicy mango sauce

These Chinese-style wontons are easy to make using ready-cooked smoked duck or chicken, or even leftovers from the Sunday roast.

MAKES ABOUT 40

15ml/1 tbsp light soy sauce
5ml/1 tsp sesame oil
2 spring onions (scallions), finely chopped
grated rind of 1/2 orange
5ml/1 tsp brown sugar
275g/10oz/1 1/2 cups chopped smoked duck
about 40 small wonton wrappers
15ml/1 tbsp vegetable oil
whole fresh chives, to garnish (optional)

FOR THE MANGO SAUCE

30ml/2 tbsp vegetable oil
5ml/1 tsp ground cumin
2.5ml/1/2 tsp ground cardamom
1.5ml/1/4 tsp ground cinnamon
250ml/8fl oz/1 cup mango purée (made
    from 1 large mango)
15ml/1 tbsp clear honey
2.5ml/1/2 tsp Chinese chilli sauce (or to taste)
15ml/1 tbsp cider vinegar
snipped fresh chives, to garnish

1 First prepare the sauce. In a medium pan, heat the oil over a medium-low heat. Add the ground cumin, cardamom and cinnamon and cook for about 3 minutes, stirring constantly.

2 Stir in the mango purée, honey, chilli sauce and vinegar. Remove from the heat and leave to cool. Pour into a bowl and cover until ready to serve.

3 Prepare the wonton filling. In a large bowl, mix together the soy sauce, sesame oil, spring onions, orange rind and brown sugar until well blended. Add the duck and toss to coat well.

4 Place a teaspoonful of the duck mixture in the centre of each wonton wrapper. Brush the edges with water and then draw them up to the centre, twisting to seal and form a pouch shape.

5 Preheat the oven to 190°F/375°C/Gas 5. Line a large baking sheet with foil and brush lightly with oil. Arrange the wontons on the baking sheet and bake for 10–12 minutes until crisp and golden. Serve with the mango sauce garnished with snipped fresh chives. If you wish, tie each wonton with a fresh chive.

Nutritional information per portion: Energy 95kcal/404kJ; Protein 6.8g; Carbohydrate 14.7g, of which sugars 0.4g; Fat 1.9g, of which saturates 0.4g; Cholesterol 28mg; Calcium 35mg; Fibre 0.7g; Sodium 36mg.

Cheese aigrettes

Choux pastry is often associated with sweet pastries, such as profiteroles, but these little savoury buns, flavoured with Gruyère and dusted with grated Parmesan, are just delicious.

MAKES 30

90g/3¹/₂ oz/scant 1 cup strong white
   bread flour
2.5ml/¹/₂ tsp paprika
2.5ml/¹/₂ tsp salt
75g/3oz/6 tbsp cold butter, diced
200ml/7fl oz/scant 1 cup water
3 eggs, beaten
75g/3oz mature Gruyère cheese,
   coarsely grated
corn or vegetable oil, for deep-frying
50g/2oz/²/₃ cup freshly grated
   Parmesan cheese
ground black pepper

1 Mix the flour, paprika and salt together by sifting them on to a large sheet of greaseproof paper. Add a generous amount of ground black pepper.

2 Put the diced butter and water into a medium pan and heat gently. As soon as the butter has melted and the liquid starts to boil, quickly tip in all the seasoned flour at once and beat very hard with a wooden spoon until the dough comes away cleanly from the sides of the pan.

3 Remove the pan from the heat and cool the paste for 5 minutes. Gradually beat in enough of the beaten egg to give a stiff dropping consistency that still holds a shape on the spoon. Mix in the Gruyère.

4 Heat the oil for deep-frying to 180°C/350°F. Take a teaspoonful of the choux paste and use a second spoon to slide it into the oil. Make more aigrettes in the same way. Fry for 3–4 minutes then drain on kitchen paper and keep warm while cooking successive batches. To serve, pile the aigrettes on a warmed serving dish and sprinkle with Parmesan.

Nutritional information per portion: Energy 84kcal/348kJ; Protein 2.2g; Carbohydrate 2.4g, of which sugars 0.1g; Fat 7.3g, of which saturates 2.7g; Cholesterol 28mg; Calcium 46mg; Fibre 0.1g; Sodium 58mg.

Parmesan thins

These thin, crisp, savoury biscuits will melt in the mouth, so make plenty for guests. They are a great snack at any time of the day, not just for parties.

MAKES 16–20

50g/2oz/¹/₂ cup plain (all-purpose) flour
40g/1¹/₂ oz/3 tbsp butter, softened
1 egg yolk
40g/1¹/₂ oz/²/₃ cup freshly grated
   Parmesan cheese
pinch of salt
pinch of mustard powder

1 Rub together the flour and the butter in a bowl using your fingertips, then work in the egg yolk, Parmesan cheese, salt and mustard. Mix to bring the dough together into a ball. Shape the mixture into a log, wrap in foil or clear film and chill in the fridge for 10 minutes.

2 Preheat the oven to 200°C/400°F/Gas 6. Cut the Parmesan log into very thin slices, 3–6mm/¹/₈–¹/₄in maximum, and arrange on a baking sheet. Flatten with a fork to give a pretty ridged pattern. Bake for 10 minutes or until the biscuits are crisp but not changing colour.

Nutritional information per portion: Energy 36kcal/148kJ; Protein 1.2g; Carbohydrate 2g, of which sugars 0.1g; Fat 2.6g, of which saturates 1.5g; Cholesterol 16mg; Calcium 29mg; Fibre 0.1g; Sodium 34mg.

Spicy peanut balls

Tasty rice balls, rolled in chopped peanuts and deep-fried, make a delicious starter. Serve them as they are, or with a chilli sauce for dipping. Make sure there are plenty of napkins to hand.

MAKES 16

1cm/¹/₂ in piece fresh root ginger
1 garlic clove, crushed
1.5ml/¹/₄ tsp turmeric
5ml/1 tsp sugar
2.5ml/¹/₂ tsp salt
5ml/1 tsp chilli sauce
10ml/2 tsp fish sauce or soy sauce
30ml/2 tbsp chopped fresh coriander
    (cilantro)
juice of ¹/₂ lime
225g/8oz/2 cups cooked white long
    grain rice
115g/4oz/1 cup peanuts, chopped
vegetable oil, for deep-frying
lime wedges and chilli sauce, to serve

1 Peel and chop the ginger and process with the garlic and turmeric in a food processor or blender until the mixture forms a smooth paste. Add the sugar, salt, chilli sauce and fish sauce or soy sauce, with the chopped fresh coriander and lime juice. Process again briefly to mix the ingredients.

2 Add three-quarters of the cooked rice to the paste and process until smooth and sticky. Scrape into a mixing bowl and stir in the remainder of the rice. Wet your hands and shape the mixture into thumb-size balls.

3 Roll the balls in the chopped peanuts, making sure they are evenly coated.

4 Heat the oil in a deep-fryer or wok. Deep-fry the peanut balls until crisp. Drain on kitchen paper and then pile on to a platter. Serve the peanut balls hot with lime wedges and chilli sauce.

Nutritional information per portion: Energy 123kcal/512kJ; Protein 2.9g; Carbohydrate 12.4g, of which sugars 0.8g; Fat 6.8g, of which saturates 1g; Cholesterol 0mg; Calcium 7mg; Fibre 0.4g; Sodium 45mg.

Pickled quail's eggs

These Chinese eggs are pickled in alcohol and can be stored in a preserving jar in a cool dark place for several months. They make delicious bitesize snacks at a drinks party.

SERVES 12

12 quail's eggs
15ml/1 tbsp salt
750ml/1¼ pints/3 cups distilled or
　previously boiled water
15ml/1 tsp Sichuan peppercorns
150ml/¼ pint/⅔ cup spirit such as
　Mou-tal (Chinese brandy), brandy,
　whisky, rum or vodka
dipping sauce and toasted sesame seeds,
　to serve

1 Boil the quail's eggs for about 4 minutes until the yolks are soft but not too runny.

2 In a large saucepan, dissolve the salt in the distilled or previously boiled water. Add the peppercorns, then allow the water to cool and add the spirit.

3 Gently tap the eggs all over but do not peel them. Place in a large, airtight, sterilized jar and fill up with the liquid, totally covering the eggs. Seal the jar and then leave the eggs to stand in a cool, dark place for 7–8 days.

4 To serve, remove the eggs from the liquid and peel off the shells carefully. Cut each egg in half or quarters and serve whole with a dipping sauce and a bowl of toasted sesame seeds.

Nutritional information per portion: Energy 20kcal/82kJ; Protein 1.7g; Carbohydrate 0g, of which sugars 0g; Fat 1.5g, of which saturates 0.4g; Cholesterol 51mg; Calcium 8mg; Fibre 0g; Sodium 19mg.

Crispy spring rolls

These small and dainty spring rolls are ideal served as appetizers or as cocktail snacks. If liked, you could replace the mushrooms with chicken or pork, and the carrots with prawns.

MAKES 40 ROLLS

225g/8oz fresh beansprouts
115g/4oz small leeks
115g/4oz carrots
115g/4oz bamboo shoots, sliced
115g/4oz mushrooms
45–60ml/3–4 tbsp vegetable oil
5ml/1 tsp salt

5ml/1 tsp light brown sugar
15ml/1 tbsp light soy sauce
15ml/1 tbsp Chinese rice wine or dry sherry
20 frozen spring roll skins, defrosted
15ml/1 tbsp cornflour (cornstarch) paste
flour, for dusting
oil, for deep-frying

1 Cut all the vegetables into thin shreds, roughly the same size and shape as the beansprouts.

2 Heat the vegetable oil in a wok and stir-fry the vegetables for about 1 minute. Add the salt, sugar, soy sauce and wine or sherry and continue stirring the vegetables for 1¹/₂–2 minutes. Remove and drain away the excess liquid, then leave to cool.

3 To make the spring rolls, cut each spring roll skin in half diagonally, then place about a tablespoonful of the vegetable mixture one-third of the way down on the skin, with the triangle pointing away from you.

4 Lift the lower edge over the filling and roll once. Fold in both ends and roll once more, then brush the upper pointed edge with a little cornflour paste, made by mixing together 4 parts cornflour with about 5 parts cold water until smooth, and roll into a neat package. Lightly dust a tray with flour and place the spring rolls on the tray with the flapside underneath.

5 To cook, heat the oil in a wok or deep-fryer until hot, then reduce the heat to low. Deep-fry the spring rolls in batches (about 8–10 at a time) for 2–3 minutes or until golden and crispy, then remove and drain. Serve the spring rolls hot with a dipping sauce, such as soy sauce, or mixed salt and pepper.

Nutritional information per portion: Energy 38kcal/161kJ; Protein 1.1g; Carbohydrate 6.6g, of which sugars 0.6g; Fat 1g, of which saturates 0.1g; Cholesterol 0mg; Calcium 15mg; Fibre 0.5g; Sodium 88mg.

Tapenade and quail's eggs

A purée made from capers, olives and anchovies, tapenade is popular in Mediterranean cooking. It complements the taste of eggs perfectly, especially quail's eggs.

SERVES 8

8 quail's eggs

1 small baguette

45ml/3 tbsp tapenade

frisée lettuce

3 small tomatoes, sliced

black olives, pitted

4 canned anchovy fillets, drained and
    halved lengthways

a little chopped parsley, to garnish

1 Boil the quail's eggs for 3 minutes, then plunge them straight into cold water to cool. Crack the shells and remove them very carefully.

2 Cut the baguette into slices on the diagonal and spread each one with some of the tapenade.

3 Arrange a little frisée lettuce, torn to fit, and the tomato slices on top. Halve the quail's eggs and place them on top of the tomato slices.

4 Quarter the olives, place one quarter on each and finally add the anchovies. Garnish with parsley.

Nutritional information per portion: Energy 157kcal/666kJ; Protein 6.3g; Carbohydrate 28.4g, of which sugars 1.8g; Fat 2.8g, of which saturates 0.6g; Cholesterol 37mg; Calcium 76mg; Fibre 1.5g; Sodium 523mg.

Eggy Thai fish cakes

These tangy little fish cakes, with a kick of Eastern spice, make great party food, dipped in an Oriental-style sauce. If they are made slightly larger, they are a great appetizer, too.

MAKES ABOUT 20

225g/8oz smoked cod or haddock (undyed)

225g/8oz fresh cod or haddock

1 small fresh red chilli

2 garlic cloves, grated

1 lemon grass stalk, very finely chopped

2 large spring onions (scallions), chopped

30ml/2 tbsp Thai fish sauce (or 30ml/ 2 tbsp soy sauce and a few drops anchovy essence)

60ml/4 tbsp thick coconut milk

2 large (US extra large) eggs, lightly beaten

15ml/1 tbsp chopped fresh coriander (cilantro)

15ml/1 tbsp cornflour (cornstarch)

oil, for frying

soy sauce, rice vinegar or Thai fish sauce, for dipping

1 Place the smoked fish in water and leave to soak for 10 minutes. Dry on kitchen paper. Roughly chop the smoked and fresh fish and place in a food processor.

2 Seed and finely chop the chilli, then add with the garlic, lemon grass, spring onions, the sauce and the coconut milk, and process until well blended with the fish. Add the eggs and coriander and process for a few more seconds. Cover with clear film (plastic wrap) and chill in the fridge for 1 hour.

3 To make the fish cakes, flour your hands with cornflour and shape teaspoonfuls of the mixture into neat balls, then coat them with flour.

4 Heat 5–7.5cm/2–3in oil in a medium pan until a crust of bread turns golden in about 1 minute. Fry the fish balls 5–6 at a time, turning them carefully for 2–3 minutes, until they turn golden all over. Remove with a slotted spoon and drain on kitchen paper. Keep the fish cakes warm until all are cooked. Serve with dipping sauces.

Nutritional information per portion: Energy 60kcal/250kJ; Protein 6.2g; Carbohydrate 0.9g, of which sugars 0.2g; Fat 3.5g, of which saturates 0.5g; Cholesterol 29mg; Calcium 15mg; Fibre 0.1g; Sodium 152mg.

Samosas

Throughout the East, these tasty snacks are sold by street vendors and eaten at any time of day. Filo pastry can be used to produce a lighter, flakier texture.

MAKES ABOUT 20

1 packet 25cm/10in spring roll wrappers
30ml/2 tbsp plain (all-purpose) flour,
   mixed with water
vegetable oil, for deep frying
coriander (cilantro) leaves, to garnish

FOR THE FILLING

25g/1oz/2 tbsp ghee or unsalted butter
1 small onion, finely chopped
1cm/½in piece fresh root ginger, peeled
   and chopped
1 garlic clove, crushed
2.5ml/½ tsp chilli powder
1 large potato, about 225g/8oz, cooked
   until just tender and finely diced
50g/2oz/½ cup cauliflower florets,
   lightly cooked, chopped small
50g/2oz/½ cup frozen peas, thawed
5–10ml/1–2 tsp garam masala
15ml/1 tbsp chopped fresh coriander
squeeze of lemon juice
salt

1 Heat the ghee or butter in a large frying pan and fry the onion, ginger and garlic for 5 minutes until the onion has softened. Add the chilli powder and cook for 1 minute, then stir in the potato, cauliflower and peas. Sprinkle with garam masala and set aside. Stir in the coriander, lemon juice and salt.

2 Cut the spring roll wrappers into three strips (or two for larger samosas). Brush the edges with a little flour paste. Place a small spoonful of filling about 2cm/¾in in from the edge of one strip.

3 Fold one corner over the filling to make a triangle and continue folding until the strip has been used and a triangular pastry has been formed. Seal any open edges with the paste.

4 Heat the oil to 190°C/375°F and deep-fry the samosas, a few at a time, until golden. Drain on kitchen paper.

5 Serve hot, garnished with the coriander.

Nutritional information per portion: Energy 56kcal/235kJ; Protein 1.3g; Carbohydrate 10g, of which sugars 0.8g; Fat 1.4g, of which saturates 0.2g; Cholesterol 0mg; Calcium 16mg; Fibre 0.7g; Sodium 8mg.

Chorizo pastry puffs

These flaky pastry puffs make a really superb accompaniment to a glass of cold sherry or beer. For best results, choose a mild cheese, as the chorizo has plenty of flavour.

SERVES 8

225g/8oz puff pastry, thawed if frozen
115g/4oz cured chorizo sausage,
    finely chopped
50g/2oz/¹⁄₂ cup grated cheese
1 small (US medium) egg, beaten
5ml/1 tsp paprika

1 Roll out the pastry thinly on a floured work surface. Using a 7.5cm/3in cutter, stamp out 16 rounds.

2 Preheat the oven to 230°C/450°F/Gas 8. Put the chopped chorizo sausage and grated cheese in a bowl and toss together lightly.

3 Lay one of the pastry rounds in the palm of your hand and place a little of the chorizo mixture across the centre. Using your other hand, pinch the edges of the pastry together along the top to seal. Repeat the process with the remaining rounds to make 16 puffs in all.

4 Place the pastries on a non-stick baking sheet and brush lightly with the beaten egg. Dust the tops of the pastries lightly with a little paprika.

5 Bake the pastries in the oven for 10–12 minutes, until puffed and golden. Serve the chorizo pastry puffs warm, dusted with the remaining paprika.

Nutritional information per portion: Energy 183kcal/763kJ; Protein 5.4g; Carbohydrate 12.1g, of which sugars 0.6g; Fat 13.1g, of which saturates 3g; Cholesterol 36mg; Calcium 73mg; Fibre 0.1g; Sodium 258mg.

Grilled asparagus with salt-cured ham

This is a very simple but delicious dish. Serve this tapas when asparagus is plentiful and not too expensive. If you can't find Serrano ham, use Italian prosciutto or Portuguese presunto.

SERVES 4

6 slices of Serrano ham
12 asparagus spears
15ml/1 tbsp olive oil
sea salt and coarsely ground black pepper

1 Preheat the grill to high. Halve each slice of the ham lengthways and wrap one half around each of the asparagus spears.

2 Brush the ham and asparagus lightly with the olive oil and sprinkle with the salt and coarsely ground black pepper.

3 Place under the grill (broiler). Grill for 5–6 minutes, turning frequently, until the asparagus is tender but still firm. Serve immediately.

Nutritional information per portion: Energy 73kcal/305kJ; Protein 7.1g; Carbohydrate 2g, of which sugars 1.9g; Fat 4.1g, of which saturates 0.8g; Cholesterol 15mg; Calcium 26mg; Fibre 1.5g; Sodium 301mg.

Prawn toasts

These crunchy sesame-topped toasts are simple to prepare and make an ideal quick appetizer, using a food processor to prepare the topping.

MAKES 64

225g/8oz cooked, peeled prawns (shrimp), well drained and patted dry
1 egg white
2 spring onions (scallions), chopped
5ml/1 tsp chopped fresh root ginger
1 garlic clove, chopped
5ml/1 tsp cornflour (cornstarch)
2.5ml/¹/₂ tsp salt
2.5ml/¹/₂ tsp sugar
2–3 dashes hot pepper sauce
8 slices firm-textured white bread
60–75ml/4–5 tbsp sesame seeds
vegetable oil, for frying
shredded spring onion, to garnish

1 Put the first nine ingredients in the bowl of a food processor and process until the mixture forms a smooth paste, scraping down the side of the bowl from time to time.

2 Spread the paste over the bread slices, then sprinkle over the sesame seeds, pressing to make them stick. Remove the crusts, then cut each slice diagonally into four triangles, and each in half again. Make 64 triangles in total.

3 Heat 5cm/2in vegetable oil in a heavy pan or wok, until hot but not smoking. Fry the triangles in batches for about 30–60 seconds, turning the toasts once. Drain on paper towels and keep hot in the oven while you cook the rest. Serve hot with the spring onion.

Nutritional information per portion: Energy 194kcal/814kJ; Protein 12.1g; Carbohydrate 28.1g, of which sugars 5.2g; Fat 3.8g, of which saturates 0.6g; Cholesterol 98mg; Calcium 108mg; Fibre 0.9g; Sodium 217mg.

Five-spice rib-sticker

Spicy and sweet sticky ribs are a popular choice in Chinese restaurants. Here, you can create your own, but make sure you choose the meatiest spare ribs you can, to make them a real success.

SERVES 8

1kg/2¼ lb pork spare ribs
10ml/2 tsp Chinese five-spice powder
2 garlic cloves, crushed
15ml/1 tbsp grated fresh root ginger
2.5ml/½ tsp chilli sauce
60ml/ 4 tbsp muscovado
    (molasses) sugar
15ml/1 tbsp sunflower oil
4 spring onions (scallions)

1 If the spare ribs are still joined together, cut between them to separate them (or ask your butcher to do this). Place the spare ribs in a large bowl.

2 Mix together all the remaining ingredients, except the spring onions, and pour over the ribs. Toss well to coat evenly. Cover the bowl and leave to marinate in the fridge overnight.

3 Cook the spare ribs under a preheated medium-hot grill (broiler), turning frequently, for 30–40 minutes. Brush occasionally with the marinade.

4 While the ribs are cooking, finely slice the spring onions – on the diagonal. To serve, place the ribs on a serving plate then scatter the spring onions over the top.

Nutritional information per portion: Energy 309kcal/1297kJ; Protein 38.3g; Carbohydrate 8g, of which sugars 8g; Fat 14g, of which saturates 4.7g; Cholesterol 123mg; Calcium 46mg; Fibre 0.1g; Sodium 75mg.

Skewered lamb with red onion salsa

This summery tapas dish is ideal for outdoor eating, although, if the weather fails, the skewers can be cooked indoors rather than barbecued. The salsa makes a refreshing accompaniment.

SERVES 4

225g/8oz lean lamb, cubed
2.5ml/¹/₂ tsp ground cumin
5ml/1 tsp paprika
15ml/1 tbsp olive oil
salt and ground black pepper

FOR THE SALSA

1 red onion, very thinly sliced
1 large tomato, seeded and chopped
15ml/1 tbsp red wine vinegar
3–4 fresh basil or mint leaves,
   coarsely torn
small mint leaves, to garnish

1 Place the lamb in a bowl with the cumin, paprika, olive oil and plenty of salt and pepper. Toss well until the lamb is coated with spices.

2 Cover the bowl with clear film (plastic wrap). Set aside in a cool place for a few hours, or in the fridge overnight, so that the lamb absorbs the flavours.

3 Spear the lamb cubes on four small skewers – if using wooden skewers, soak first in cold water for 30 minutes to prevent them from burning.

4 To make the salsa, put the sliced onion, tomato, red wine vinegar and basil or mint leaves in a small bowl and stir together until thoroughly blended. Season to taste with salt, garnish with mint, then set aside while you cook the lamb skewers.

5 Cook on a barbecue or under a preheated grill (broiler) for 5–10 minutes, turning frequently, until the lamb is well browned but still slightly pink in the centre. Serve hot, with the salsa.

Nutritional information per portion: Energy 135kcal/563kJ; Protein 11.4g; Carbohydrate 2g, of which sugars 1.6g; Fat 9.2g, of which saturates 3.4g; Cholesterol 43mg; Calcium 10mg; Fibre 0.5g; Sodium 51mg.

Soups, pâtés and terrines

There are endless possibilities for making

soup and the recipes here range from a

light Hot-and-Sour Soup to the hearty

Vermicelli Soup. Pâtés and terrines are

great for impressing your guests. Try

the Grilled Vegetable Terrine, which

looks stunning, or the deliciously rich

Chicken Liver Pâté.

Gazpacho with avocado salsa

Tomatoes, cucumber and peppers form the basis of this classic, chilled soup. Add a spoonful of chunky, fresh avocado salsa and a scattering of croûtons for a delicious summer starter. This is quite a substantial soup, so follow with a light main course, such as grilled fish or chicken.

SERVES 4–6

2 slices day-old bread
600ml/1 pint/2¹⁄₂ cups chilled water
1kg/2¹⁄₄ lb tomatoes
1 cucumber
1 red (bell) pepper, seeded and chopped
1 green chilli, seeded and chopped
2 garlic cloves, chopped
30ml/2 tbsp extra virgin olive oil
juice of 1 lime and 1 lemon
few drops of Tabasco sauce
salt and ground black pepper

handful of fresh basil, to garnish
8–12 ice cubes, to serve

FOR THE CROÛTONS
2–3 slices day-old bread, crusts removed
1 garlic clove, halved
15–30ml/1–2 tbsp olive oil

FOR THE AVOCADO SALSA
1 ripe avocado
5ml/1 tsp lemon juice
2.5cm/1in piece cucumber, diced
¹⁄₂ red chilli, finely chopped

1 Make the soup first. In a shallow bowl, soak the day-old bread in 150ml/¹⁄₄ pint/²⁄₃ cup of the chilled water for 5 minutes.

2 Meanwhile, place the tomatoes in a heatproof bowl; cover with boiling water. Leave for 30 seconds, then peel, seed and chop the flesh.

3 Thinly peel the cucumber, cut in half lengthways and scoop out the seeds with a teaspoon. Discard the seeds and chop the flesh.

4 Place the bread, tomatoes, cucumber, red pepper, chilli, garlic, oil, citrus juices, Tabasco and the remaining chilled water in a food processor or blender. Blend until mixed but still chunky. Season and chill well.

5 To make the croûtons, rub the slices of bread with the cut surface of the garlic clove. Cut the bread into cubes and place in a plastic bag with the olive oil. Seal the bag and shake until the bread cubes are coated with the oil. Heat a large non-stick frying pan and fry the croûtons over a medium heat until crisp and golden.

6 Just before serving make the avocado salsa. Halve the avocado, remove the stone (pit), then peel and dice the flesh. Toss the avocado in the lemon juice to prevent it browning, then mix with the cucumber and chilli.

7 Ladle the soup into bowls, add the ice cubes, and top with a spoonful of avocado salsa. Garnish with the basil and hand round the croûtons separately.

COOK'S TIP
For a superior flavour choose Haas avocados with the rough-textured, almost black skins.

Nutritional information per portion: Energy 164kcal/685kJ; Protein 3.5g; Carbohydrate 16.6g, of which sugars 7.9g; Fat 9.7g, of which saturates 1.7g; Cholesterol 0mg; Calcium 40mg; Fibre 3.1g; Sodium 112mg.

Chilled prawn and cucumber soup

If you've never served a chilled soup before, this is the one to try first. Delicious and light, it's the perfect way to celebrate summer. Try crab meat, or cooked, flaked salmon fillet as an alternative.

SERVES 4

25g/1oz/2 tbsp butter
2 shallots, finely chopped
2 garlic cloves, crushed
1 cucumber, peeled, seeded and diced
300ml/1/2 pint/1 1/4 cups milk
225g/8oz cooked peeled prawns (shrimp)
15ml/1 tbsp each finely chopped fresh
    mint, dill, chives and chervil
300ml/1/2 pint/1 1/4 cups whipping cream
salt and ground white pepper

FOR THE GARNISH

30ml/2 tbsp crème fraîche or sour
    cream (optional)
4 large, cooked prawns (shrimp), peeled
    with tail intact
fresh chives and dill

1 Melt the butter in a pan and cook the shallots and garlic over a low heat until soft but not coloured. Add the cucumber and cook the vegetables gently, stirring frequently, until tender.

2 Stir in the milk, bring almost to the boil, then lower the heat and simmer for 5 minutes. Tip the soup into a blender or food processor and purée until it is very smooth. Season to taste with salt and ground white pepper.

3 Pour the soup into a bowl and set aside to cool. When cool, stir in the prawns, chopped herbs and the whipping cream. Cover, then transfer the soup to the fridge and chill for at least 2 hours.

4 To serve, ladle the soup into four individual bowls and top each portion with a dollop of crème fraîche or sour cream, if using. Place a prawn over the edge of each dish. Garnish with the fresh chives and dill.

Nutritional information per portion: Energy 439kcal/1817kJ; Protein 18.9g; Carbohydrate 7.5g, of which sugars 7.1g; Fat 37.2g, of which saturates 23.1g; Cholesterol 255mg; Calcium 212mg; Fibre 0.5g; Sodium 245mg.

Hot-and-sour soup

This light and invigorating soup originates from Thailand. It is traditionally served at the beginning of a formal Thai meal to stimulate the appetite.

SERVES 4

2 carrots
900ml/1½ pints/3¾ cups
   vegetable stock
2 Thai chillies, seeded and finely sliced
2 lemon grass stalks, outer leaves
   removed and each stalk cut
   into 3 pieces
4 kaffir lime leaves
2 garlic cloves, finely chopped
4 spring onions (scallions), finely sliced
5ml/1 tsp sugar
juice of 1 lime
45ml/3 tbsp chopped fresh coriander
   (cilantro)
salt, to taste
130g/4½ oz/1 cup Japanese tofu, sliced

1 To make carrot flowers, cut each carrot in half crossways, then, using a small sharp knife, cut four V-shaped channels lengthways. Slice the carrots into thin rounds and set aside.

2 Pour the vegetable stock into a saucepan. Reserve 2.5ml/½ tsp of the chillies and add the rest to the pan with the lemon grass pieces, the lime leaves, garlic and half the spring onions. Bring the mixture to the boil, then reduce the heat and

simmer for 20 minutes. Remove from the heat, strain the stock and discard the flavourings.

3 Return the stock to the pan, add the reserved chillies and spring onions, the sugar, lime juice, coriander and salt to taste.

4 Simmer for 5 minutes, then add the carrot flowers and tofu slices, and cook the soup for a further 2 minutes until the carrot is just tender. Serve hot.

Nutritional information per portion: Energy 43kcal/180kJ; Protein 3.4g; Carbohydrate 3.9g, of which sugars 3.6g; Fat 1.7g, of which saturates 0.2g; Cholesterol 0mg; Calcium 202mg; Fibre 1.4g; Sodium 13mg.

Spanish garlic soup

This is a simple and satisfying soup, which is based on one of the most popular ingredients that is used in the Mediterranean region – garlic!

SERVES 4

30ml/2 tbsp olive oil

4 large garlic cloves, peeled

4 slices French bread, 5mm/¼in thick

15ml/1 tbsp paprika

1 litre/1¾ pints/4 cups beef stock

1.5ml/¼ tsp ground cumin

pinch of saffron threads

4 eggs

salt and ground black pepper

chopped fresh parsley, to garnish

1 Preheat the oven to 230°C/450°F/Gas 8. Heat the oil in a large pan. Add the whole garlic cloves and cook until golden. Remove and set aside. Fry the bread in the oil until golden, then set aside.

2 Add the paprika to the pan, and fry for a few seconds, stirring. Stir in the beef stock, the cumin and saffron, then add the reserved fried garlic, crushing the cloves with the back of a wooden spoon. Season with salt and ground black pepper then cook for about 5 minutes.

3 Ladle the soup into four ovenproof bowls and gently break an egg into each one. Place the slices of fried French bread on top of the eggs and place in the oven for about 3–4 minutes, or until the eggs are set. Sprinkle with chopped fresh parsley and serve immediately.

COOK'S TIP
Use home-made beef stock for the best flavour or buy prepared stock from your supermarket – you'll find it in the chilled counter. Never use stock cubes as they contain too much salt.

Nutritional information per portion: Energy 253kcal/1061kJ; Protein 11.8g; Carbohydrate 26.5g, of which sugars 1.5g; Fat 12g, of which saturates 2.5g; Cholesterol 190mg; Calcium 82mg; Fibre 2g; Sodium 318mg.

Soya beansprout soup

This soup has a hint of spiciness and a refreshing nutty flavour. It is quick and easy to make and is reputed to have a calming effect on the stomach.

SERVES 4

200g/7 oz/generous 2 cups soya
    beansprouts
1 red or green chilli
15 dried anchovies
1 spring onion (scallion), finely sliced
3 garlic cloves, chopped
salt

1 Wash the soya beansprouts and trim off the tail ends.

2 Halve and seed the chilli and cut it diagonally into thin slices.

3 Add 750ml/1¼ pints/3 cups water to a pan with the dried anchovies. Bring to the boil. After boiling for 15 minutes remove the anchovies and discard them.

4 Add the soya beansprouts and boil for 5 minutes, ensuring the lid is kept tightly on the pan. Add the spring onion, sliced chilli and garlic, and boil for a further 3 minutes. Add salt to taste, and serve.

Nutritional information per portion: Energy 41kcal/173kJ; Protein 4.6g; Carbohydrate 2.7g, of which sugars 1.2g; Fat 1.4g, of which saturates 0.2g; Cholesterol 7mg; Calcium 46mg; Fibre 1g; Sodium 445mg.

Spinach and tofu soup

This soup is really delicious as well as being very quick to make. If fresh spinach is not in season, watercress or lettuce can be used as an alternative.

SERVES 4

1 x 200g/7oz block tofu
115g/4oz spinach leaves
750ml/1¼ pints/3 cups vegetable stock
15ml/1 tbsp light soy sauce
salt and ground black pepper

1 Rinse the tofu then cut into 12 small pieces, each about 5mm/¼in thick. Wash the spinach leaves thoroughly and cut them into small pieces.

2 In a wok or large pan, bring the stock to a rolling boil. Add the tofu and soy sauce, bring back to the boil and simmer for about 2 minutes.

3 Add the spinach and simmer for a further minute. Skim the surface, then add salt and ground black pepper to taste, and serve.

Nutritional information per portion: Energy 50kcal/208kJ; Protein 5.5g; Carbohydrate 1.2g, of which sugars 0.9g; Fat 2.6g, of which saturates 0.3g; Cholesterol 0mg; Calcium 337mg; Fibre 0.6g; Sodium 310mg.

Avocado soup

This is a simple but delicious soup. To add a subtle garlic flavour, rub the cut side of a garlic clove around the soup bowls before adding the soup.

SERVES 4

2 large ripe avocados
1 litre/1³⁄₄ pints/4 cups chicken stock
250ml/8fl oz/1 cup single (light) cream
salt and ground white pepper
15ml/1 tbsp finely chopped coriander
   (cilantro), to garnish (optional)

1 Cut the avocados in half, remove the stones and mash the flesh. Put the flesh into a sieve and using a wooden spoon, press the avocado through into a warmed bowl.

2 Heat the chicken stock with the cream in a saucepan. When the mixture is hot, but not boiling, whisk it into the puréed avocado.

3 Season to taste with salt and pepper. Serve immediately, sprinkled with the coriander, if using. The soup may be served chilled, if liked.

COOK'S TIP
Avocados are ripe when they yield slightly if gently pressed at the stalk end.

Nutritional information per portion: Energy 263kcal/1087kJ; Protein 3.5g; Carbohydrate 2.8g, of which sugars 1.8g; Fat 26.4g, of which saturates 10.7g; Cholesterol 34mg; Calcium 64mg; Fibre 2.6g; Sodium 23mg.

Vermicelli soup

This hearty soup brings a taste of the Mediterranean to the table. The inclusion of fresh coriander adds a piquancy to this soup and complements the tomato flavour.

SERVES 4

30ml/2 tbsp olive or corn oil
50g/2oz vermicelli
1 onion, roughly chopped
1 garlic clove, chopped
450g/1lb tomatoes, peeled, seeded and
   roughly chopped
1 litre/1³⁄₄ pints/4 cups chicken stock
1.5ml/¼ tsp sugar
15ml/1 tbsp finely chopped
   fresh coriander (cilantro)
salt and ground black pepper
chopped fresh coriander (cilantro),
   to garnish
25g/1oz/¼ cup freshly grated Parmesan
   cheese, to serve

1 Heat the oil in a frying pan and sauté the vermicelli over a moderate heat until golden brown. Move it about continuously to avoid burning. Remove the vermicelli with a slotted spoon or tongs and drain on kitchen paper.

2 Purée the onion, garlic and tomatoes in a food processor or blender until smooth. Return the frying pan to the heat. When the oil is hot again, add the purée to the pan. Cook, stirring constantly to prevent sticking, for about 5 minutes or until thick.

3 Transfer the purée to a saucepan. Add the vermicelli and pour in the stock. Season with sugar, salt and pepper. Stir in the coriander, bring to the boil, then lower the heat, cover the pan and simmer the soup gently until the vermicelli is tender.

4 Serve in warmed soup bowls, sprinkle with chopped fresh coriander and offer the grated Parmesan cheese separately.

Nutritional information per portion: Energy 141kcal/589kJ; Protein 4.4g; Carbohydrate 13.3g, of which sugars 3.5g; Fat 7.9g, of which saturates 2.2g; Cholesterol 6mg; Calcium 86mg; Fibre 1.1g; Sodium 79mg.

Baby carrot and fennel soup

Sweet tender carrots find their moment of glory in this delicately spiced soup. Fennel provides a subtle aniseed flavour that does not overpower the carrots.

SERVES 4

50g/2oz/4 tbsp butter
1 small bunch spring onions (scallions),
   chopped
150g/5oz fennel bulb, chopped
1 celery stick, chopped
450g/1lb new carrots, grated
2.5ml/¹/₂ tsp ground cumin

150g/5oz new potatoes, peeled and diced
1.2 litres/2 pints/5 cups chicken or
   vegetable stock
60ml/4 tbsp double (heavy) cream
salt and ground black pepper
60ml/4 tbsp chopped fresh parsley,
   to garnish

1 Melt the butter in a large pan and add the spring onions, fennel, celery, carrots and cumin. Cover and cook for about 5 minutes, or until soft.

2 Add the diced potatoes and chicken or vegetable stock, and simmer the mixture for a further 10 minutes.

3 Liquidize the soup in the pan with a hand-held blender. Stir in the cream and season to taste. Serve in individual soup bowls and garnish with chopped parsley and fennel leaves.

COOK'S TIP
For convenience, you can freeze the soup before adding the cream, seasoning and parsley.

Nutritional information per portion: Energy 244kcal/1010kJ; Protein 2.5g; Carbohydrate 16.8g, of which sugars 10.6g; Fat 19g, of which saturates 11.7g; Cholesterol 47mg; Calcium 62mg; Fibre 4.4g; Sodium 122mg.

Chilled asparagus soup

This soup provides a delightful way to enjoy a favourite seasonal vegetable. Choose bright, crisp-looking asparagus with firm, slender stalks for the best effect.

SERVES 6

900g/2lb fresh asparagus
60ml/4 tbsp olive oil
**175g/6oz/1¹/₂ cups sliced leeks or
    spring onions (scallions)**
45ml/3 tbsp flour
**1.5 litres/2¹/₂ pints/6¹/₄ cups chicken
    stock or water**
**120ml/4fl oz/¹/₂ cup single (light) cream
    or natural (plain) yogurt**
salt and ground black pepper
**15ml/1 tbsp minced fresh tarragon
    or chervil**

1 Cut the top 6cm/2¹/₂in off the asparagus spears. Blanch these tips in boiling water for 5-6 minutes until they are just tender. Drain. Cut each tip into 2 or 3 pieces, and set aside. Trim the ends of the stalks, removing any brown or woody parts. Chop the asparagus stalks into 1cm/¹/₂in pieces.

2 Heat the olive oil in a heavy pan. Add the leeks or spring onions and cook over a low heat for 5–8 minutes, until softened. Stir in the chopped asparagus stalks, cover and cook for a further 6–8 minutes. Add the flour and stir well. Cook for 3–4 minutes, uncovered, stirring occasionally. Add the stock or water and bring to the boil, stirring frequently, then reduce the heat and simmer for 30 minutes. Season the soup to taste with salt and pepper.

3 Purée the soup in a food processor or blender and strain, if necessary. Stir in the tips, most of the cream or yogurt, and the herbs. Cool then chill well. To serve, stir well, season and garnish with the remaining cream or yogurt.

Nutritional information per portion: Energy 163kcal/676kJ; Protein 6.4g; Carbohydrate 10.2g, of which sugars 4.3g; Fat 11g, of which saturates 6.5g; Cholesterol 27mg; Calcium 82mg; Fibre 3.2g; Sodium 54mg.

Fresh tomato soup

Intensely flavoured sun-ripened tomatoes need little embellishment in this fresh-tasting soup.
On a hot day, this Italian soup is also delicious chilled.

SERVES 6

1.3–1.6kg/3–3¹/₂ lb ripe tomatoes
400ml/14fl oz/1²/₃ cups chicken or
   vegetable stock
45ml/3 tbsp sun-dried tomato paste
30–45ml/2–3 tbsp balsamic vinegar
10–15ml/2–3 tsp caster (superfine) sugar
small handful of basil leaves, plus extra
   to garnish
salt and ground black pepper
toasted cheese croûtes and crème
   fraîche, to serve

1 Plunge the tomatoes into boiling water for 30 seconds, then refresh in cold water. Peel away the skins and quarter the tomatoes. Put them in a large saucepan and pour over the chicken or vegetable stock. Bring just to the boil, reduce the heat, cover and simmer the mixture gently for 10 minutes until the tomatoes are pulpy.

2 Stir in the tomato paste, vinegar, sugar and basil. Season with salt and pepper, then cook gently, stirring, for 2 minutes. Process the soup in a blender or food processor, then return to the pan and reheat gently. Serve in bowls topped with one or two toasted cheese croûtes and a spoonful of crème fraîche, garnished with basil leaves.

Nutritional information per portion: Energy 49kcal/210kJ; Protein 1.9g; Carbohydrate 9.5g, of which sugars 9.5g; Fat 0.7g, of which saturates 0.2g; Cholesterol 0mg; Calcium 19mg; Fibre 2.4g; Sodium 38mg.

Malayan prawn laksa

This spicy prawn and noodle soup tastes just as good when made with fresh crab meat or any flaked, cooked fish. You can also use ready-made laksa paste, available from specialist stores.

SERVES 3–4

115g/4oz rice vermicelli or stir-fry
   rice noodles
15ml/1 tbsp vegetable or groundnut oil
600ml/1 pint/2¹/₂ cups fish stock
400ml/14fl oz/1²/₃ cups thin
   coconut milk
30ml/2 tbsp Thai fish sauce
¹/₂ lime
16–24 cooked peeled prawns (shrimp)
salt and cayenne pepper
60ml/4 tbsp fresh coriander (cilantro)
   sprigs and leaves, chopped, to garnish

FOR THE SPICY PASTE

2 lemon grass stalks, finely chopped
2 fresh red chillies, seeded and chopped
2.5cm/1in piece fresh root ginger, peeled
   and sliced
2.5ml/¹/₂ tsp dried shrimp paste
2 garlic cloves, chopped
2.5ml/¹/₂ tsp ground turmeric
30ml/2 tbsp tamarind paste

1 Cook the rice vermicelli in a large pan of boiling salted water according to the instructions on the packet. Tip into a large sieve or colander, then rinse under cold water and drain. Set aside and keep warm.

2 To make the spicy paste, place all the ingredients in a mortar and pound with a pestle. Or, if you prefer, put the ingredients in a food processor or blender and then process until a smooth paste is formed.

3 Heat the oil in a large pan, add the paste and fry, stirring constantly, for a few moments to release the flavours, but be careful not to let it burn. Add the fish stock and coconut milk and bring to the boil. Stir in the fish sauce, then simmer for 5 minutes. Season with salt and cayenne to taste, adding a squeeze of lime. Add the prawns and heat through for a few seconds.

4 Divide the noodles among three or four soup plates. Pour the soup over, making sure that each portion includes an equal number of prawns. Garnish with coriander and serve piping hot.

Nutritional information per portion: Energy 194kcal/814kJ; Protein 12.1g; Carbohydrate 28.1g, of which sugars 5.2g; Fat 3.8g, of which saturates 0.6g; Cholesterol 98mg; Calcium 108mg; Fibre 0.9g; Sodium 217mg.

Tortellini chanterelle broth

The savoury-sweet quality of chanterelle mushrooms combines well in a simple broth with spinach-and-ricotta-filled tortellini. The sherry adds a lovely warming effect.

SERVES 4

350g/12oz fresh spinach and ricotta
 tortellini, or 175g/6oz dried
1.2 litres/2 pints/5 cups chicken stock
75ml/5 tbsp dry sherry
175g/6oz fresh chanterelle mushrooms,
 trimmed and sliced, or 15g/¹/₂ oz/
 ¹/₂ cup dried chanterelles
chopped fresh parsley, to garnish

1 Cook the tortellini according to the packet instructions. Bring the chicken stock to the boil, add the dry sherry and fresh or dried mushrooms and then simmer for 10 minutes.

2 Strain the tortellini, add to the stock, then ladle the broth into four warmed bowls, making sure each contains the same proportions of tortellini and mushrooms. Garnish with the chopped parsley and serve.

Nutritional information per portion: Energy 204kcal/859kJ; Protein 7.6g; Carbohydrate 23.4g, of which sugars 1.5g; Fat 4.3g, of which saturates 0.1g; Cholesterol 0mg; Calcium 106mg; Fibre 1.6g; Sodium 185mg.

Curried parsnip soup

The spices, which impart a delicious, mild curry flavour that carries an exotic breath of India, are the perfect way to bring out the sweetness of the parsnips.

SERVES 4

25g/1oz/2 tbsp butter
1 garlic clove, crushed
1 onion, chopped
5ml/1 tsp ground cumin
5ml/1 tsp ground coriander
4 parsnips, peeled and sliced
10ml/2 tsp medium curry paste
450ml/³⁄₄ pint/scant 2 cups chicken stock
450ml/³⁄₄ pint/scant 2 cups milk
60ml/4 tbsp sour cream
squeeze of lemon juice
salt and ground black pepper
fresh chives, to garnish
bread, to serve

1 Heat the butter in a large pan and add the garlic and onion. Fry gently for 4–5 minutes, until lightly golden. Stir in the cumin and coriander and cook for a further 1–2 minutes.

2 Add the parsnips and stir until well coated with the butter, then stir in the curry paste, followed by the stock. Cover the pan and simmer for 15 minutes, until the parsnips are tender.

3 Ladle the soup into a blender or food processor and process until smooth. Return the soup to the pan and stir in the milk. Heat gently for 2–3 minutes, then add half the sour cream and all the lemon juice. Season well. Serve in bowls topped with swirls of the remaining sour cream and the chopped fresh chives, accompanied by the bread.

Nutritional information per portion: Energy 150kcal/623kJ; Protein 4.7g; Carbohydrate 7.8g, of which sugars 6.8g; Fat 11.4g, of which saturates 7g; Cholesterol 32mg; Calcium 170mg; Fibre 0.8g; Sodium 112mg.

Split pea soup

This tasty winter soup is a perfect family starter, and is great for cooking when you have lots of left-over food, such as cold ham and vegetables, from the holidays.

SERVES 4–6

25g/1oz/2 tbsp butter
1 large onion, chopped
1 large celery stick with leaves, chopped
2 carrots, chopped
1 smoked gammon (smoked or cured
    ham) knuckle, 450g/1lb
2 litres/3¹⁄₂ pints/8¹⁄₂ cups water
350g/12oz/1¹⁄₂ cups split peas
30ml/2 tbsp chopped fresh parsley,
    plus extra to garnish
2.5ml/¹⁄₂ tsp dried thyme
1 bay leaf
about 30ml/2 tbsp lemon juice
salt and ground black pepper

1 Melt the butter in a large heavy pan. Add the onion, celery and carrots and cook until soft, stirring occasionally.

2 Place all the remaining ingredients in the pan. Bring to the boil, cover and simmer gently for 2 hours.

3 After 2 hours, once the peas are very tender, remove the gammon knuckle. Leave it to cool a bit, then remove the skin and cut the meat away from the bones. Discard the skin and bones, then cut the meat into chunks as evenly sized as possible.

4 Return the chunks of gammon to the soup. Discard the bay leaf. Taste and adjust the seasoning with more lemon juice, salt and pepper. Serve hot, sprinkled with fresh parsley.

Nutritional information per portion: Energy 244kcal/1033kJ; Protein 17.2g; Carbohydrate 35.2g, of which sugars 3.4g; Fat 4.8g, of which saturates 2.5g; Cholesterol 19mg; Calcium 40mg; Fibre 3.5g; Sodium 254mg.

French onion and morel soup

French onion soup is appreciated for its light beefy taste. Few improvements can be made to this classic soup, but some richly scented morel mushrooms will impart an intense, savoury flavour.

SERVES 4

50g/2oz/4 tbsp unsalted butter, plus
    extra for spreading
15ml/1 tbsp vegetable oil
3 onions, sliced
900ml/1¹/₂ pints/3³/₄ cups beef stock
75ml/5 tbsp Madeira or sherry
8 dried morel mushrooms
4 slices French bread
75g/3oz Gruyère, Beaufort or Fontina
    cheese, grated
30ml/2 tbsp chopped fresh parsley

1 Melt the butter with the oil in a large frying pan, then add the sliced onions and cook gently for 10–15 minutes until the onions are a rich mahogany brown colour.

2 Transfer the browned onions to a large pan, cover with beef stock, add the Madeira or sherry and the dried morels, then simmer for 20 minutes.

3 Preheat the grill (broiler) to a moderate temperature and toast the French bread on both sides. Spread one side with butter and heap with the grated cheese. Ladle the soup into four flameproof bowls, float the cheesy toasts on top and grill (broil) until they are crisp and brown. Alternatively, grill (broil) the cheese-topped toast, then place one slice in each warmed soup bowl before ladling the hot soup over it. The toast will float to the surface. Scatter over the chopped fresh parsley and serve.

Nutritional information per portion: Energy 304kcal/1263kJ; Protein 8.8g; Carbohydrate 22.6g, of which sugars 8g; Fat 20.1g, of which saturates 10.9g; Cholesterol 45mg; Calcium 225mg; Fibre 2.8g; Sodium 349mg.

Wild mushroom soup

Wild mushrooms are expensive, but dried porcini have a concentrated flavour, so only a small quantity is needed. The beef stock helps to strengthen the earthy taste of the mushrooms.

SERVES 4

25g/1oz/1 cup dried porcini mushrooms
30ml/2 tbsp olive oil
15g/¹/₂ oz/1 tbsp butter
2 each leeks and shallots, thinly sliced
1 garlic clove, roughly chopped
225g/8oz/3 cups fresh wild mushrooms

about 1.2 litres/2 pints/5 cups beef stock
2.5ml/¹/₂ tsp dried thyme
150ml/¹/₄ pint/²/₃ cup double
   (heavy) cream
salt and ground black pepper
thyme sprigs, to garnish

1 Put the dried porcini in a bowl, add 250ml/8fl oz/1 cup warm water and leave to soak for 20–30 minutes. Lift out of the liquid and squeeze over the bowl to remove as much of the soaking liquid as possible. Strain all the liquid and reserve to use later. Finely chop the porcini.

2 Heat the oil and butter in a large saucepan until foaming. Add the sliced leeks, chopped shallots and garlic and cook gently for about 5 minutes, stirring frequently, until soft.

3 Chop or slice the fresh wild mushrooms and add to the pan. Stir over a medium heat for a few minutes until they begin to soften. Pour in the stock and bring to the boil. Add the porcini, their soaking liquid, the dried thyme and salt and ground black pepper. Lower the heat, half cover the pan and simmer the soup gently for 30 minutes, stirring occasionally.

4 Pour about three-quarters of the soup into a blender or food processor and process until very smooth. Return the purée to the soup remaining in the pan, stir in the cream and heat through. Check the consistency and add a little more stock or water if the soup is too thick. Taste for seasoning. Serve hot garnished with thyme sprigs.

Nutritional information per portion: Energy 287kcal/1183kJ; Protein 2.6g; Carbohydrate 3.5g, of which sugars 2.7g; Fat 29.3g, of which saturates 15.4g; Cholesterol 59mg; Calcium 38mg; Fibre 1.9g; Sodium 35mg.

Spinach and rice soup

Use very fresh, young spinach leaves in the preparation of this light and fresh-tasting soup. If you cannot find Pecorino cheese, you can use the slightly milder tasting Parmesan instead.

SERVES 4

675g/1½ lb fresh spinach, washed
45ml/3 tbsp extra virgin olive oil
1 small onion, finely chopped
2 garlic cloves, finely chopped
1 small fresh red chilli, seeded and
    finely chopped
115g/4oz/generous 1 cup risotto rice
1.2 litres/2 pints/5 cups vegetable stock
salt and ground black pepper
60ml/4 tbsp grated Pecorino cheese

1 Place the spinach in a large pan with just the water that clings to its leaves after washing. Add a large pinch of salt. Heat gently until the spinach has wilted, then remove from the heat and drain, reserving any liquid.

2 Either chop the spinach finely using a large knife or place in a food processor and process to a fairly coarse purée.

3 Heat the oil in a large saucepan and gently cook the onion, garlic and chilli for 4–5 minutes until softened. Stir in the rice until well coated, then pour in the stock and reserved spinach liquid. Bring to the boil, lower the heat and simmer for 10 minutes. Add the spinach, with salt and pepper to taste.

4 Cook for a further 5–7 minutes, until the rice is tender. Check the seasoning and adjust if needed. Serve with the Pecorino cheese.

Nutritional information per portion: Energy 293kcal/1215kJ; Protein 13g; Carbohydrate 26.8g, of which sugars 3.4g; Fat 14.7g, of which saturates 4.4g; Cholesterol 15mg; Calcium 476mg; Fibre 3.8g; Sodium 400mg.

Broccoli soup with garlic toast

This is an Italian recipe, originating from Rome. For the best flavour and colour, use the freshest broccoli you can find and a good-quality Parmesan cheese, such as Parmigiano-Reggiano.

SERVES 6

675g/1¹/₂ lb broccoli spears
1.75 litres/3 pints/7¹/₂ cups chicken or
  vegetable stock
salt and ground black pepper
30ml/2 tbsp fresh lemon juice
freshly grated Parmesan cheese
  (optional), to serve

FOR THE GARLIC TOAST
6 slices white bread
1 large garlic clove, halved

1 Using a small sharp knife, peel the broccoli stems, starting from the base of the stalks and pulling gently up towards the florets. (The peel comes off very easily.) Chop the broccoli into small chunks.

2 Bring the stock to the boil in a large pan. Add the chopped broccoli and simmer for 20 minutes, or until soft.

3 Purée about half of the soup in a blender or food processor and then mix into the rest of the soup. Season with salt, pepper and lemon juice.

4 Just before serving, reheat the soup to just below boiling point. Toast the bread, rub with garlic and cut into quarters. Place 3 or 4 pieces of toast in the base of each soup plate. Ladle on the soup. Serve at once, with grated Parmesan cheese, if using.

Nutritional information per portion: Energy 98kcal/413kJ; Protein 7.2g; Carbohydrate 14.0g, of which sugars 2.4g, Fat 1.5g, of which saturates 0.2g; Cholesterol 0mg; Calcium 91mg; Fibre 3.4g; Sodium 139mg.

Chilled tomato and sweet pepper soup

This recipe was inspired by the most well-known chilled soup, Spanish gazpacho. However, the difference is that this soup is cooked first, then chilled.

SERVES 4

2 red (bell) peppers, halved, cored and seeded
45ml/3 tbsp olive oil
1 onion, finely chopped
2 garlic cloves, crushed
675g/1¹/₂ lb ripe well-flavoured tomatoes
150ml/¹/₄ pint/²/₃ cup red wine
600ml/1 pint/2¹/₂ cups chicken stock

salt and ground black pepper
chopped fresh chives, to garnish

FOR THE CROÛTONS

2 slices white bread, crusts removed
60ml/4 tbsp olive oil

1 Cut each red pepper half into quarters. Place skin-side up on a grill (broiler) rack and cook until the skins are charred. Transfer to a bowl and cover with a plate or pop into a plastic bag and seal.

2 Heat the oil in a large pan. Add the onion and garlic and cook gently until soft. Meanwhile, remove the skin from the peppers and roughly chop the flesh. Cut the tomatoes into chunks.

3 Add the peppers and tomatoes to the pan, then cover and cook gently for 10 minutes. Add the wine and cook for a further 5 minutes, then add the stock and salt and pepper and continue to simmer for 20 minutes.

4 To make the croûtons, cut the bread into cubes. Heat the oil in a small frying pan, add the bread and fry until golden. Drain on kitchen paper and store in an airtight box once cool.

5 Process the soup in a blender or food processor until smooth. Pour into a clean glass or ceramic bowl and leave to cool thoroughly before chilling in the fridge for at least 3 hours. When the soup is cold, season to taste.

6 Serve the soup in bowls, topped with the croûtons and garnished with chopped chives.

Nutritional information per portion: Energy 292kcal/1216kJ; Protein 3.4g; Carbohydrate 18.8g, of which sugars 11.8g; Fat 20.4g, of which saturates 3g; Cholesterol 0mg; Calcium 40mg; Fibre 3.5g; Sodium 92mg.

Smoked haddock pâté

Arbroath smokies are small haddock that are beheaded and gutted, but not split, before being salted and hot-smoked, creating a great flavour.

SERVES 6

butter, for greasing
3 large Arbroath smokies, about
    225g/8oz each
275g/10oz/1¼ cups soft white
    (farmer's cheese)
3 eggs, beaten
30–45ml/2–3 tbsp lemon juice
ground black pepper
chervil sprigs, to garnish
lemon wedges and lettuce leaves,
    to serve

1 Preheat the oven to 160°C/325°F/Gas 3. Carefully butter six ramekin dishes.

2 Lay the smokies in an ovenproof dish and heat through in the oven for 10 minutes. Carefully remove the skin and bones from the smokies, then flake the flesh into a bowl.

3 Mash the fish with a fork and work in the cheese, then the eggs. Add lemon juice and pepper.

4 Divide the fish mixture equally among the ramekins and place in a roasting pan. Pour hot water into the roasting pan to come halfway up the dishes. Bake for 30 minutes, until just set.

5 Allow to cool for 2–3 minutes, then run a knife point around the edge of each dish and invert on to a warmed plate. Garnish with chervil sprigs and serve with the lemon wedges and lettuce.

Nutritional information per portion: Energy 307kcal/1274kJ; Protein 22.2g; Carbohydrate 1.5g, of which sugars 1.5g; Fat 23.7g, of which saturates 7.3g; Cholesterol 166mg; Calcium 59mg; Fibre 0g; Sodium 723mg.

Smoked salmon pâté

This pâté is made in individual ramekins lined with smoked salmon so that it looks really special.
Taste the mousse as you are making it, and add more lemon juice and seasoning if necessary.

SERVES 4

350g/12oz thinly sliced smoked salmon
  (wild if possible)
150ml/¼ pint/²/₃ cup double
  (heavy) cream
finely grated rind and juice of 1 lemon
salt and ground black pepper
melba toast, to serve

1 Line four small ramekin dishes with clear film (plastic wrap). Then line the dishes with 115g/4oz of the smoked salmon cut into strips long enough to flop over the edges.

2 In a food processor fitted with a metal blade, process the rest of the salmon with the double cream, lemon rind and juice, salt and plenty of ground black pepper.

3 Pack the lined ramekins with the smoked salmon pâté and wrap over the loose strips of salmon. Cover the ramekins with clear film and chill for 30 minutes. Invert on to plates; serve with Melba toast.

Nutritional information per portion: Energy 311kcal/1293kJ; Protein 22.9g; Carbohydrate 0.8g, of which sugars 0.8g; Fat 24.1g, of which saturates 13.2g; Cholesterol 82mg; Calcium 36mg; Fibre 0g; Sodium 1654mg.

Herbed liver pâté pie

Serve this highly flavoured pâté with a glass of Pilsner beer for a change from wine, and some spicy dill pickles to complement the strong tastes.

SERVES 10

675g/1½ lb minced pork
350g/12oz pork liver
350g/12oz/2 cups diced cooked ham
1 small onion, finely chopped
30ml/2 tbsp chopped fresh parsley
5ml/1 tsp German mustard
30ml/2 tbsp Kirsch
5ml/1 tsp salt
beaten egg, for sealing and glazing
25g/1oz sachet aspic jelly
250ml/8fl oz/1 cup boiling water
ground black pepper
mustard, bread and dill pickles, to serve

FOR THE PASTRY

450g/1lb/4 cups plain (all-purpose) flour
275g/10oz/1¼ cups butter
2 eggs plus 1 egg yolk
30ml/2 tbsp water

1 Preheat the oven to 200°C/400°F/ Gas 6. For the pastry, sift the flour and salt and rub in the butter. Beat the eggs, egg yolk and water, and mix into the flour. Knead the dough until smooth. Roll out two-thirds on a lightly floured surface and use to line a 10 x 25cm/4 x 10in hinged loaf tin. Trim any excess dough.

2 Process half the pork and all of the liver until fairly smooth. Stir in the remaining pork, ham, onion, parsley, mustard, Kirsch, salt and black pepper. Spoon into the tin and level the surface.

3 Roll out the remaining pastry and use it to top the pie. Seal the edges with egg. Decorate with pastry trimmings and glaze with egg. Make 4 holes in the top. Bake for 40 minutes, turn the oven down to 180°C/350°F/Gas 4 and cook for another hour. Cover with foil. Cool in the tin.

4 Make up the aspic jelly with the boiling water. Dissolve, then cool. Make a small hole near the pie edge and pour in the aspic. Chill for 2 hours. Serve in slices with mustard, bread and dill pickles.

Nutritional information per portion: Energy 576kcal/2407kJ; Protein 32.9g; Carbohydrate 36g, of which sugars 1.6g; Fat 33.7g, of which saturates 18.1g; Cholesterol 273mg; Calcium 87mg; Fibre 1.5g; Sodium 888mg.

Chicken liver pâté

This rich-tasting, smooth pâté will keep in the fridge for about 3 days. Serve with thick slices of hot toast or warmed bread – a rustic olive oil bread such as ciabatta would be a good partner.

SERVES 8

115g/4oz chicken livers, thawed if frozen, trimmed
1 small garlic clove, chopped
15ml/1 tbsp sherry
30ml/2 tbsp brandy
50g/2oz/¼ cup butter, melted
2.5ml/¼ tsp salt
fresh herbs and black peppercorns, to garnish
hot toast or warmed bread, to serve

1 Preheat the oven to 150°C/300°F/Gas 2. Place the chicken livers and chopped garlic in a food processor or blender and process until they are smooth.

2 With the motor running, gradually add the sherry, brandy, melted butter and salt.

3 Pour the liver mixture into two 7.5cm/3in ramekins. Cover the tops with foil but do not allow the foil to come down the sides too far.

4 Place the ramekins in a small roasting pan and carefully pour in boiling water so that it comes to about halfway up the sides of the ramekins.

5 Carefully transfer the pan to the oven and bake the pâté for 20 minutes. Leave to cool to room temperature, then remove the ramekins from the pan and chill until needed. Serve the pâté with toast or bread, garnished with herbs and peppercorns.

Nutritional information per portion: Energy 70kcal/290kJ; Protein 2.6g; Carbohydrate 0.1g, of which sugars 0.1g; Fat 5.5g, of which saturates 3.4g; Cholesterol 68mg; Calcium 2mg; Fibre 0g; Sodium 49mg.

Sea trout mousse

This deliciously creamy mousse makes a little sea trout go a long way. It is equally good when made with salmon. Serve with crisp Melba toast or triangles of lightly toasted pitta bread.

SERVES 6

250g/9oz sea trout fillet
120ml/4fl oz/¹/₂ cup fish stock
2 gelatine leaves, or 15ml/1 tbsp
    powdered gelatine
juice of ¹/₂ lemon
30ml/2 tbsp dry sherry or dry vermouth
30ml/2 tbsp freshly grated Parmesan
300ml/¹/₂ pint/1¹/₄ cups whipping cream

2 egg whites
15ml/1 tbsp sunflower oil, for greasing
salt and ground white pepper

FOR THE GARNISH
5cm/2in piece cucumber, with peel, thinly
    sliced and halved
fresh dill or chervil, chopped

1 Put the sea trout in a shallow pan. Pour in the stock and heat to simmering point. Poach the fish for 3–4 minutes, until it is lightly cooked. Strain the stock into a jug and leave the trout to cool slightly.

2 Add the gelatine to the hot stock and stir until it has dissolved completely. Set aside until required.

3 When the trout is cool enough to handle, remove the skin and flake the flesh into a bowl. Pour the stock into a food processor or blender. Process briefly, then gradually add the flaked trout, lemon juice, sherry or vermouth and grated Parmesan, continuing to process the mixture until it is smooth. Scrape the mixture into a large bowl and leave to cool completely.

4 Lightly whip the cream in a bowl; fold it into the cold trout mixture. Season to taste, then cover with clear film (plastic wrap) and chill in the fridge until the mousse is just starting to set. In a grease-free bowl, beat the egg whites with a pinch of salt until they are softly peaking. Using a metal spoon, stir about one-third into the fish mixture to slacken it slightly, then fold in the rest.

5 Lightly grease six ramekins or similar individual serving dishes. Divide the mousse among the prepared dishes and level the surface. Place in the fridge for 2–3 hours, until set. Just before serving, arrange a few slices of cucumber and a herb sprig on top and scatter over a little dill or chervil.

Nutritional information per portion: Energy 241kcal/999kJ; Protein 12.3g; Carbohydrate 1.8g, of which sugars 1.8g; Fat 20g, of which saturates 14.5g; Cholesterol 9mg; Calcium 104mg; Fibre 0.1g; Sodium 127mg.

Salmon rillettes

This economical way of serving salmon, with only one little fillet required per head, makes an impressive starter and can be made in advance and stored in the fridge.

SERVES 6

350g/12oz salmon fillets
175g/6oz/³/₄ cup butter, softened
1 celery stick, finely chopped
1 leek, white part only, finely chopped
1 bay leaf
150ml/¹/₄ pint/²/₃ cup dry white wine

115g/4oz smoked salmon trimmings
generous pinch of ground mace
60ml/4 tbsp fromage frais (low-fat cream cheese)
salt and ground black pepper
salad leaves, to serve

1 Lightly season the salmon. Melt 25g/1oz/2 tbsp of the butter in a medium heavy pan. Add the celery and leek and cook for about 5 minutes. Add the salmon and bay leaf and pour the white wine over. Cover and cook for about 15 minutes until tender.

2 Strain the cooking liquid into a pan and boil until reduced to 30ml/2 tbsp. Cool. Meanwhile, melt 50g/2oz/4 tbsp of the remaining butter and gently cook the smoked salmon trimmings until they turn pale pink. Leave to cool.

3 Remove the skin and any bones from the salmon fillets. Flake the flesh into a bowl and add the reduced, cooled cooking liquid.

4 Beat in the remaining butter, with the ground mace and the fromage frais. Break up the cooked smoked salmon trimmings and fold into the salmon mixture with all the juices from the pan. Taste and adjust the seasoning if you need to.

5 Spoon the salmon mixture into a dish or terrine and smooth the top level. Cover with clear film (plastic wrap) and chill. The prepared mixture can be left in the fridge for up to 2 days.

6 To serve the salmon rillettes, shape the mixture into oval quenelles using two dessert spoons and arrange on individual plates with the salad leaves. Accompany the rillettes with brown bread or oatcakes, if you like.

Nutritional information per portion: Energy 370kcal/1530kJ; Protein 17.2g; Carbohydrate 0.9g, of which sugars 0.7g; Fat 31.4g, of which saturates 16.5g; Cholesterol 98mg; Calcium 30mg; Fibre 0.4g; Sodium 568mg.

Potted salmon with lemon and dill

This sophisticated starter would be ideal for a dinner party. Preparation is done well in advance, so you can concentrate on the main course. If you cannot find fresh dill, use dried dill.

SERVES 6

350g/12oz cooked salmon, skinned
150g/5oz/²/₃ cup butter, softened
rind and juice of 1 large lemon
10ml/2 tsp chopped fresh dill
salt and ground white pepper
75g/3oz/³/₄ cup flaked (sliced) almonds,
    roughly chopped

1 Flake the salmon into a bowl and then place in a food processor together with two-thirds of the butter, the lemon rind and juice, half the dill, and plenty of salt and pepper. Blend until the mixture is quite smooth.

2 Mix in the flaked almonds. Check the seasoning and pack the mixture into small ramekins.

3 Scatter the other half of the dill over the top of each ramekin. Clarify the remaining butter, and pour over each ramekin to make a seal. Chill. Serve with crudités.

Nutritional information per portion: Energy 370kcal/1531kJ; Protein 14.8g; Carbohydrate 1.2g, of which sugars 0.9g; Fat 34.1g, of which saturates 14.7g; Cholesterol 82mg; Calcium 64mg; Fibre 1.4g; Sodium 182mg.

Potted prawns

The tiny brown prawns that were traditionally used for potting are very fiddly to peel. Since they are rare nowadays, it is easier to use peeled, cooked prawns instead.

SERVES 4

225g/8oz/2 cups peeled prawns (shrimp)
225g/8oz/1 cup butter
pinch of ground mace
salt, to taste
cayenne pepper
dill sprigs, to garnish
lemon wedges and thin slices of brown
  bread and butter, to serve

1 Chop a quarter of the prawns. Melt 115g/4oz/¹/₂ cup of the butter slowly, carefully skimming off any foam that rises to the surface with a metal spoon.

2 Stir all the prawns, the mace, salt and cayenne into the pan and heat gently without boiling. Pour the prawns and butter mixture into four individual pots and leave to cool.

3 Heat the remaining butter in a clean small pan, then carefully spoon the clear butter over the prawns, leaving behind the sediment.

4 Leave until the butter is almost set, then place a dill sprig in the centre of each pot. Leave to set completely, then cover and chill.

5 Transfer the prawns to room temperature 30 minutes before serving with lemon wedges for squeezing over and thin slices of brown bread and butter.

Nutritional information per portion: Energy 461kcal/1901kJ; Protein 10.3g; Carbohydrate 0.4g, of which sugars 0.4g; Fat 46.6g, of which saturates 29.4g; Cholesterol 230mg; Calcium 55mg; Fibre 0g; Sodium 448mg.

Roast pepper terrine

This terrine is perfect for a dinner party because it tastes better if made ahead. Prepare the salsa on the day of serving. Serve with a warmed Italian bread such as ciabatta or focaccia.

SERVES 8

8 (bell) peppers (red, yellow and orange)
675g/1¹/₂ lb/3 cups mascarpone
3 eggs, separated
30ml/2 tbsp each roughly chopped flat
    leaf parsley and shredded basil
2 large garlic cloves, roughly chopped

2 red, yellow or orange (bell) peppers,
    seeded and roughly chopped
30ml/2 tbsp extra virgin olive oil
10ml/2 tsp balsamic vinegar
a few basil sprigs
salt and ground black pepper

1 Place the whole peppers under a hot grill (broiler) for 8–10 minutes, turning frequently. Then put into a plastic bag until cold before skinning and seeding them. Chop seven of the peppers lengthways into thin strips.

2 Put the mascarpone in a bowl with the egg yolks, herbs and half the garlic. Add seasoning. Beat well. In a separate bowl, whisk the egg whites to a soft peak, then fold into the cheese mixture until they are evenly incorporated.

3 Preheat the oven to 180°C/350°F/Gas 4. Line the base of a lightly oiled 900g/2lb loaf tin (pan). Put one-third of the cheese mixture in the tin and spread level. Arrange half the pepper strips on top in an even layer. Repeat until all the cheese and peppers are used, ending with a layer of the cheese mixture.

4 Cover the tin with foil and place in a roasting pan. Pour in boiling water to come halfway up the sides of the tin. Bake for 1 hour. Leave to cool in the water bath, then lift out and chill overnight.

5 A few hours before serving, make the salsa. Place the remaining skinned pepper and fresh peppers in a food processor. Add the remaining garlic, oil and vinegar. Set aside a few basil leaves for garnishing and add the rest to the processor. Process until finely chopped. Tip the mixture into a bowl, add salt and ground black pepper to taste and mix well. Cover and chill until ready to serve.

6 Turn out the terrine, peel off the lining paper and slice thickly. Garnish with the reserved basil leaves and serve cold, with the sweet pepper salsa.

Nutritional information per portion: Energy 581kcal/2425kJ; Protein 21.9g; Carbohydrate 78.1g, of which sugars 74.6g; Fat 21.8g, of which saturates 9.8g; Cholesterol 107mg; Calcium 105mg; Fibre 18.9g; Sodium 74mg.

Asparagus and egg terrine

For a special dinner this terrine is a delicious choice yet it is very light. Make the hollandaise sauce well in advance and warm through gently when required.

SERVES 8

150ml/¼ pint/²/₃ cup milk
150ml/¼ pint/²/₃ cup double
　(heavy) cream
40g/1½oz/3 tbsp butter
40g/1½oz/3 tbsp flour
75g/3oz herbed or garlic cream cheese
675g/1½ lb asparagus spears, cooked
a little oil
2 eggs, separated
15ml/1 tbsp chopped fresh chives
30ml/2 tbsp chopped fresh dill

salt and ground black pepper
dill sprigs, to garnish

**FOR THE ORANGE
HOLLANDAISE SAUCE**
15ml/1 tbsp white wine vinegar
15ml/1 tbsp fresh orange juice
4 black peppercorns
1 bay leaf
2 egg yolks
115g/4oz/½ cup butter, melted and
　cooled slightly

1 Put the milk and cream into a small pan and heat to just below boiling point. Melt the butter in a medium pan, stir in the flour and cook to a thick paste. Gradually stir in the milk, whisking as it thickens and beat to a smooth paste. Stir in the cream cheese, season to taste with salt and ground black pepper and leave to cool slightly.

2 Trim the asparagus to fit the width of a 1.2 litre/2 pint/5 cup loaf tin (pan) or terrine. Lightly oil the tin and then place a sheet of baking parchment in the base, cut to fit. Preheat the oven to 180°C/350°F/Gas 4.

3 Beat the yolks into the sauce mixture. Whisk the whites until stiff and fold in with the chives, dill and seasoning. Layer the asparagus and egg mixture in the tin, starting and finishing with asparagus. Cover the top with foil.

4 Place the terrine in a roasting pan; half fill with hot water. Cook for 45–55 minutes until firm.

5 To make the hollandaise sauce, put the vinegar, juice, peppercorns and bay leaf in a small pan and heat until reduced by half.

6 Cool the sauce slightly, then whisk in the egg yolks, then the butter, with a balloon whisk over a very gentle heat. Season to taste and keep whisking until thick. Keep the sauce warm over a pan of hot water.

7 When the terrine is just firm to the touch remove from the oven and allow to cool, then chill. Carefully invert the terrine on to a serving dish, remove the baking parchment and garnish with the dill. Cut into slices and pour over the warmed sauce.

Nutritional information per portion: Energy 359kcal/1483kJ; Protein 6.6g; Carbohydrate 7.1g, of which sugars 3.2g; Fat 34.1g, of which saturates 20.2g; Cholesterol 175mg; Calcium 87mg; Fibre 1.6g; Sodium 179mg.

Grilled vegetable terrine

A colourful, layered terrine, this appetizer uses many of the vegetables that are associated with the Mediterranean and long, balmy summer evenings.

SERVES 6

2 large red (bell) peppers, quartered,
    cored, seeded
2 large yellow (bell) peppers, quartered,
    cored, seeded
1 large aubergine (eggplant), sliced
    lengthways
2 courgettes (zucchini), sliced lengthways
90ml/6 tbsp olive oil
1 large red onion, thinly sliced
75g/3oz/1/2 cup raisins

15ml/1 tbsp tomato purée (paste)
15ml/1 tbsp red wine vinegar
400ml/14fl oz/12/3 cups tomato juice
15g/1/2oz/2 tbsp powdered gelatine
fresh basil leaves, to garnish

FOR THE DRESSING

90ml/6 tbsp extra virgin olive oil
30ml/2 tbsp red wine vinegar
salt and ground black pepper

1 Place the peppers skin-side up under a hot grill (broiler) and cook until the skins are blackened. Transfer to a bowl and cover. Leave to cool. Arrange the aubergine and courgette slices on separate baking sheets. Brush them with oil and cook under the grill, turning occasionally, until they are tender and golden.

2 Heat the remaining olive oil in a frying pan, and add the sliced onion, raisins, tomato purée and red wine vinegar. Cook gently until the mixture is soft and syrupy. Set aside and leave to cool in the frying pan.

3 Lightly oil a 1.75 litre/3 pint/71/2 cup terrine then line it with clear film (plastic wrap), leaving a little hanging over the sides. Pour half the tomato juice into a pan, and sprinkle with the gelatine. Dissolve over a low heat, stirring to prevent any lumps from forming.

4 Place a layer of red peppers in the base of the terrine, and pour in enough of the tomato juice with gelatine to cover. Continue layering the vegetables, pouring tomato juice over each layer. Finish with a layer of red peppers. Add the remaining tomato juice to the pan, and pour into the terrine. Give it a sharp tap, to disperse the juice. Cover and chill until set.

5 To make the dressing, whisk together the oil and vinegar, and season. Turn out the terrine and remove the clear film (plastic wrap). Serve in thick slices, drizzled with dressing and garnished with basil leaves.

Nutritional information per portion: Energy 296kcal/1229kJ; Protein 3.5g; Carbohydrate 20.2g, of which sugars 19.7g; Fat 22.9g, of which saturates 3.4g; Cholesterol 0mg; Calcium 42mg; Fibre 3.8g; Sodium 169mg.

Haddock and smoked salmon terrine

This is a fairly substantial terrine, so serve modest slices, perhaps with fresh dill mayonnaise or a mango salsa. You can use any thick white fish fillets, such as hoki.

SERVES 10–12

15ml/1 tbsp sunflower oil,
   for greasing
350g/12oz oak-smoked salmon
900g/2lb haddock fillets, skinned
2 eggs, lightly beaten
105ml/7 tbsp crème fraîche

30ml/2 tbsp drained capers
30ml/2 tbsp drained soft green or
   pink peppercorns
salt and ground white pepper
crème fraîche, peppercorns, fresh dill and
   rocket (arugula), to garnish

1 Preheat the oven to 200°C/400°F/Gas 6. Grease a 1 litre/1¾ pint/4 cup loaf tin (pan) or terrine with the sunflower oil. Use some of the smoked salmon to line the loaf tin or terrine, allowing some of the ends to overhang the mould. Reserve the remaining smoked salmon until needed.

2 Cut two long slices of haddock the length of the tin or terrine and set aside. Cut the rest of the haddock into small pieces. Season all of the haddock with salt and ground white pepper.

3 Combine the eggs, crème fraîche, capers and green or pink peppercorns in a bowl. Add salt and pepper; stir in the haddock pieces. Spoon the mixture into the mould until it is one-third full. Smooth the surface with a spatula.

4 Wrap the long haddock fillets in the reserved salmon. Lay them on top of the layer of the fish mixture in the tin or terrine. Cover with the rest of the fish mixture, smooth the surface and fold the overhanging pieces of salmon over the top. Cover tightly with a double thickness of foil. Tap the terrine to settle the contents. Stand the terrine in a roasting tin and pour in boiling water to come halfway up the sides. Place in the oven and cook for 45 minutes–1 hour, until the filling is just set.

5 Take the terrine out of the roasting tin, but do not remove the foil cover. Place two or three large heavy tins on the foil to weight it and leave until cold. Chill in the fridge for 24 hours. About an hour before serving, remove the terrine from the fridge, lift off the weights and remove the foil. Carefully invert on to a serving plate and garnish with crème fraîche, peppercorns and sprigs of dill and rocket leaves.

Nutritional information per portion: Energy 154kcal/647kJ; Protein 22.5g; Carbohydrate 0.3g, of which sugars 0.3g; Fat 7.1g, of which saturates 3g; Cholesterol 78mg; Calcium 34mg; Fibre 0.2g; Sodium 571mg.

Chicken and pork terrine

This pale, elegant terrine is flecked with green peppercorns and parsley, which give it a wonderfully subtle flavour. For a sharper flavour, use fresh coriander instead of parsley.

SERVES 6–8

225g/8oz rindless, streaky (fatty) bacon
375g/13oz chicken breast fillets, skinned
15ml/1 tbsp lemon juice
225g/8oz lean minced (ground) pork
1/2 small onion, finely chopped
2 eggs, beaten
30ml/2 tbsp chopped fresh parsley

5ml/1 tsp salt
5ml/1 tsp green peppercorns, crushed
oil, for greasing
salad leaves, capers, sliced gherkins and
    beetroot (beets), to serve

1 Preheat the oven to 160°C/325°F/Gas 3. Put the bacon on a board and stretch it using the back of a knife before arranging it in overlapping slices over the base and sides of a 900g/2lb loaf tin (pan).

2 Cut 115g/4oz of the chicken into strips about 10cm/4in long. Sprinkle with lemon juice. Put the rest of the chicken in a food processor or blender with the minced pork and the onion. Process until fairly smooth.

3 Add the eggs, parsley, salt and peppercorns to the meat mixture and process again briefly. Spoon half the mixture into the loaf tin and then level the surface. Arrange the chicken strips on top, then spoon in the remaining meat mixture and smooth the top. Give the tin a couple of sharp taps to knock out any pockets of air.

4 Cover the loaf tin with a piece of oiled foil and put it in a roasting pan. Pour in enough hot water to come halfway up the sides of the loaf tin. Bake for about 45–50 minutes, until firm. Allow the terrine to cool in the tin before turning out and chilling. Serve sliced, with salad leaves, capers, sliced gherkins and beetroot.

Nutritional information per portion: Energy 296kcal/1229kJ; Protein 3.5g; Carbohydrate 20.2g, of which sugars 19.7g; Fat 22.9g, of which saturates 3.4g; Cholesterol 0mg; Calcium 42mg; Fibre 3.8g; Sodium 169mg.

Vegetarian dishes

A wide variety of dishes from around the

world are included in this chapter, with

recipes from Europe to Asia. You can

transport yourself to the Far East with

Vegetable Tempura or enjoy a taste of the

Mediterranean with Greek Aubergine

and Spinach Pie.

Griddled tomatoes on soda bread

Nothing could be simpler than this delightful appetizer, yet a drizzle of olive oil and balsamic vinegar and shavings of Parmesan cheese transform it into something really rather special.

SERVES 4

olive oil, for brushing and drizzling
6 tomatoes, thickly sliced
4 thick slices soda bread
balsamic vinegar, for drizzling
salt and ground black pepper
shavings of Parmesan cheese, to serve

1 Brush a griddle pan with olive oil and heat. Add the tomato slices and cook for about 4 minutes, turning once, until softened and slightly blackened. Or, heat the grill (broiler) to high and line the rack with foil. Grill (broil) the slices for 4–6 minutes, turning once, until softened.

2 Meanwhile, lightly toast the soda bread. Place the tomatoes on top of the toast and then drizzle each portion with a little olive oil and balsamic vinegar. Season to taste with salt and black pepper and serve immediately with thin shavings of Parmesan cheese.

Nutritional information per portion: Energy 172kcal/724kJ; Protein 4g; Carbohydrate 25.1g, of which sugars 5.8g; Fat 6.9g, of which saturates 0.9g; Cholesterol 0mg; Calcium 63mg; Fibre 2.3g; Sodium 171mg.

Poached eggs Florentine

The term "à la Florentine" means "in the style of Florence" and refers to dishes cooked with spinach and topped with Mornay sauce. Here is a subtly spiced, elegant starter.

SERVES 4

675g/1½ lb spinach, washed and drained

25g/1oz/2 tbsp butter

60ml/4 tbsp double (heavy) cream

pinch of freshly grated nutmeg

salt and ground black pepper

FOR THE TOPPING

25g/1oz/2 tbsp butter

25g/1oz/¼ cup plain flour

300ml/½ pint/1¼ cups hot milk

pinch of ground mace

115g/4oz Gruyère cheese, grated

4 eggs

15ml/1 tbsp freshly grated
  Parmesan cheese, plus shavings
  to serve

1 Place the spinach in a large saucepan with very little water. Cook for 3–4 minutes or until tender, then drain and chop finely. Return the spinach to the pan, add the butter, cream, nutmeg and seasoning and heat through. Place in the base of one large or four small gratin dishes.

2 To make the topping, heat the butter in a small pan, add the flour and cook for 1 minute to a paste. Gradually blend in the hot milk, beating well as it thickens to break up any lumps.

3 Cook for 1–2 minutes, stirring. Remove from the heat and stir in the mace and three-quarters of the Gruyère cheese.

4 Preheat the oven to 200°C/ 400°F/Gas 6. Poach the eggs in lightly salted water for 3–4 minutes. Make hollows in the spinach with the back of a spoon, and place a poached egg in each one. Cover with the cheese sauce and sprinkle with the remaining Gruyère and Parmesan. Bake for 10 minutes or until golden. Serve at once with Parmesan shavings.

Nutritional information per portion: Energy 459kcal/1901kJ; Protein 21.7g; Carbohydrate 11.5g, of which sugars 6.5g; Fat 36g, of which saturates 20.3g; Cholesterol 270mg; Calcium 636mg; Fibre 3.8g; Sodium 626mg.

Dolmades

These stuffed vine leaves originated in Greece. If you can't find fresh vine leaves, use a packet or can of brined leaves. Soak in hot water for 20 minutes, then rinse and dry well on kitchen paper.

MAKES 20–24

24–28 fresh young vine leaves, soaked
30ml/2 tbsp olive oil
1 large onion, finely chopped
1 garlic clove, crushed
225g/8oz/2 cups cooked long grain rice
about 45ml/3 tbsp pine nuts
15ml/1 tbsp flaked (sliced) almonds
40g/1¹/₂ oz/¹/₄ cup sultanas
    (golden raisins)
15ml/1 tbsp snipped fresh chives
15ml/1 tbsp finely chopped fresh mint
juice of ¹/₂ lemon
150ml/¹/₄ pint/²/₃ cup white wine
hot vegetable stock
salt and ground black pepper
mint sprig, to garnish
garlic yogurt and pitta bread, to serve

1 Cook the vine leaves in boiling water for 2–3 minutes. If using packet or canned leaves, place in a bowl, cover with boiling water and leave for 20 minutes until the leaves can be separated. Rinse and pat dry.

2 Heat the oil in a frying pan and fry the onion and garlic for 3–4 minutes. Spoon into a bowl, add the cooked rice and mix. Stir in 30ml/2 tbsp of the pine nuts, the almonds, sultanas, chives and mint. Add the lemon juice, salt and pepper and mix.

3 Reserve four vine leaves. Place the rest on a work surface with the veined side uppermost and put a spoonful of filling near each stem, fold the lower part of the leaf over it, roll up and fold in the sides.

4 Line the base of a deep frying pan with the reserved vine leaves. Place the dolmades close together in the pan, seam side down, in a single layer. Pour over the wine and enough stock to just cover. Place a plate on top of the dolmades, cover the pan and simmer for 30 minutes.

5 Cool and chill, then garnish with pine nuts and mint. Serve with the garlic yogurt and some pitta bread.

Nutritional information per portion: Energy 43kcal/181kJ; Protein 0.7g; Carbohydrate 6.7g, of which sugars 1.7g; Fat 1.1g, of which saturates 0.1g; Cholesterol 0mg; Calcium 12mg; Fibre 0.3g; Sodium 2mg.

Lemon, thyme and bean stuffed mushrooms

Portabello mushrooms have a rich flavour and a meaty texture that go well with this fragrant herb-and-lemon stuffing. The pine nut accompaniment is a traditional Middle Eastern dish.

SERVES 4–6

400g/14oz/2 cups canned aduki beans
45ml/3 tbsp olive oil, plus extra
for brushing
1 onion, finely chopped
2 garlic cloves, crushed
30ml/2 tbsp fresh chopped thyme or
5ml/1 tsp dried
8 large field (portabello) mushrooms,
stalks finely chopped
50g/2oz/1 cup fresh wholemeal
(whole-wheat) breadcrumbs
juice of 1 lemon
185g/6¹/₂ oz/³/₄ cup goat's
cheese, crumbled
salt and ground black pepper

FOR THE PINE NUT SAUCE

50g/2oz/¹/₂ cup pine nuts, toasted
50g/2oz/1 cup cubed white bread
2 garlic cloves, chopped
200ml/7fl oz/scant 1 cup milk
45ml/3 tbsp olive oil

1 Rinse the beans, drain, then set aside. Preheat the oven to 200°C/400°F/Gas 6. Heat the oil in a frying pan, add the onion and garlic and sauté for 5 minutes until softened. Add the thyme and the mushroom stalks and cook for 3 minutes, stirring occasionally, until tender.

2 Add the beans, breadcrumbs and lemon juice, season, then cook for 2 minutes. Mash two-thirds of the beans.

3 Brush an ovenproof dish and the base and sides of the mushrooms with oil, then top each one with a spoonful of the bean mixture. Place the mushrooms in the dish, cover with foil and bake for 20 minutes. Remove the foil. Top the mushrooms with the goat's cheese and bake for a further 15 minutes, until the mushrooms are tender.

4 To make the sauce, place all the ingredients in a food processor or blender and blend until smooth and creamy. Add more milk if the mixture appears too thick. Serve with the stuffed mushrooms.

Nutritional information per portion: Energy 403kcal/1680kJ; Protein 17g; Carbohydrate 25.8g, of which sugars 5.8g; Fat 26.5g, of which saturates 8g; Cholesterol 31mg; Calcium 158mg; Fibre 5.8g; Sodium 572mg.

Cannellini bean and rosemary bruschetta

This is a sophisticated variation on the theme of beans on toast, which, with the addition of the Mediterranean flavours of garlic and sun-dried tomatoes, makes an unusual starter.

SERVES 6

150g/5oz/²/₃ cup dried cannellini beans
5 tomatoes
45ml/3 tbsp olive oil, plus extra
    for drizzling
2 sun-dried tomatoes in oil, drained and
    finely chopped
1 garlic clove, crushed

30ml/2 tbsp chopped fresh rosemary
12 slices Italian-style bread, such
    as ciabatta
1 large garlic clove
salt and ground black pepper
handful of fresh basil leaves, to garnish

1 Put the beans in a bowl, cover in water and soak overnight. Drain and rinse the beans, then place in a saucepan and cover with fresh water. Bring to the boil and boil rapidly for 10 minutes. Then simmer for 50–60 minutes or until tender. Drain, return to the pan and keep warm.

2 Meanwhile, place the tomatoes in a bowl, cover with boiling water; leave for 30 seconds, then peel, seed and chop the flesh. Heat the oil in a frying pan, add the fresh and sun-dried tomatoes, garlic and rosemary. Cook for 2 minutes until the tomatoes begin to break down and soften.

3 Add the tomato mixture to the cannellini beans and season to taste. Mix together well. Keep the bean mixture warm.

4 Rub the cut sides of the bread slices with the garlic clove, then toast them lightly. Spoon the cannellini bean mixture on top of the toast. Sprinkle with basil leaves and drizzle with a little extra olive oil before serving.

Nutritional information per portion: Energy 499kcal/2111kJ; Protein 20.2g; Carbohydrate 84.3g, of which sugars 8.5g; Fat 11.3g, of which saturates 1.7g; Cholesterol 0mg; Calcium 195mg; Fibre 8.1g; Sodium 749mg.

Glamorgan sausages

These tasty sausages, which are flavoured with herbs and mustard are ideal for vegetarians as they are made from cheese and leeks rather than meat.

MAKES 8

150g/5oz/2½ cups fresh breadcrumbs
150g/5oz generous cup grated
   Caerphilly cheese
1 small leek, very finely chopped
15ml/1 tbsp chopped fresh parsley
leaves from 1 thyme sprig, chopped
2 eggs
7.5ml/1½ tsp English (hot) mustard powder
about 45ml/3 tbsp milk
plain (all-purpose) flour, for coating
15ml/1 tbsp oil
15g/½ oz/1 tbsp butter, melted
salt and ground black pepper
salad leaves and tomato halves, to serve

1 Mix the breadcrumbs, cheese, leek, herbs and seasoning. Whisk the eggs with the mustard and reserve 30ml/2 tbsp. Stir the rest into the cheese mixture with enough milk to bind.

2 Divide the cheese mixture into eight portions and then form them into sausage shapes.

3 Dip the sausages in the reserved egg to coat. Season the flour, then roll the sausages in it to give a light, even coating. Chill for about 30 minutes until they are firm.

4 Preheat the grill (broiler) and oil the rack. Mix the oil and melted butter together and use to brush over the sausages. Cook the sausages for 5–10 minutes, turning them carefully every now and then, until golden brown all over. Serve hot or cold, with salad leaves and tomato halves.

Nutritional information per portion: Energy 193kcal/809kJ; Protein 8.8g; Carbohydrate 15.1g, of which sugars 0.9g; Fat 10.9g, of which saturates 5.7g; Cholesterol 70mg; Calcium 179mg; Fibre 0.8g; Sodium 309mg.

Potato skewers with mustard dip

Potatoes cooked on the barbecue have a great flavour and crisp skin. Try these delicious kebabs served with a thick, garlic-rich dip for an unusual start to a meal.

SERVES 6

FOR THE DIP

4 garlic cloves, crushed

2 egg yolks

30ml/2 tbsp lemon juice

300ml/1/2 pint/1¼ cups extra virgin
   olive oil

10ml/2 tsp wholegrain mustard

salt and ground black pepper

FOR THE SKEWERS

1kg/2¼ lb small new potatoes

200g/7oz shallots, halved

30ml/2 tbsp olive oil

15ml/1 tbsp sea salt

1 Prepare the barbecue, or preheat the grill (broiler). To make the dip place the garlic, egg yolks and lemon juice in a blender or a food processor fitted with a metal blade and process for just a few seconds until the mixture is smooth.

2 Keep the blender motor running and add the oil very gradually, pouring it in a thin stream, until the mixture forms a thick, glossy cream. Add the mustard and stir the ingredients together, then season with salt and pepper. Chill until ready to use.

3 Par-boil the potatoes in their skins in boiling water for 5 minutes. Drain well and then thread them on to metal skewers alternating with the shallots.

4 Brush the skewers with oil and sprinkle with salt. Barbecue or grill (broil) for about 10–12 minutes, turning occasionally. Serve with the mustard dip.

Nutritional information per portion: Energy 488kcal/2024kJ; Protein 4.3g; Carbohydrate 29.5g, of which sugars 4.1g; Fat 40g, of which saturates 6.1g; Cholesterol 65mg; Calcium 28mg; Fibre 2.2g; Sodium 49mg.

Deep-fried new potatoes with saffron aioli

Serve these crispy little golden potatoes dipped into a wickedly garlicky mayonnaise – then sit back and watch them disappear in a matter of minutes!

SERVES 4

1 egg yolk
2.5ml/¹⁄₂ tsp Dijon mustard
300ml/¹⁄₂ pint/1¹⁄₄ cups extra virgin olive oil
15–30ml/1–2 tbsp lemon juice
1 garlic clove, crushed
2.5ml/¹⁄₂ tsp saffron threads
20 baby, new or salad potatoes
vegetable oil, for deep-frying
salt and ground black pepper

1 For the saffron aioli, put the egg yolk in a bowl with the Dijon mustard and a pinch of salt. Stir to mix together well. Beat in the olive oil very slowly, drop by drop at first and then in a very thin stream. Stir in the lemon juice.

2 Season the aioli with salt and pepper then add the crushed garlic and beat into the mixture thoroughly to combine.

3 Place the saffron in a small bowl and add 10ml/2 tsp hot water. Press the saffron threads with the back of a teaspoon, to extract the colour and flavour, and leave to infuse for 5 minutes. Beat the saffron and the liquid into the aioli.

4 Cook the potatoes in their skins in boiling salted water for 5 minutes, then turn off the heat. Cover the pan and leave for 15 minutes. Drain the potatoes, then dry them thoroughly in a dish towel.

5 Heat a 1cm/¹⁄₂in layer of vegetable oil in a deep pan. When the oil is very hot, add the potatoes and fry quickly, turning them constantly, until crisp and golden all over. Drain well on kitchen paper and then serve them hot with the saffron aioli.

Nutritional information per portion: Energy 788kcal/3266kJ; Protein 5g; Carbohydrate 40.3g, of which sugars 3.3g; Fat 68.6g, of which saturates 9.7g; Cholesterol 50mg; Calcium 21mg; Fibre 2.5g; Sodium 30mg.

Asparagus with raspberry dressing

The flavours of asparagus and raspberries complement each other wonderfully well. The tangy, fruity sauce gives this starter a real zing and the bright colours make it very attractive.

SERVES 4

675g/1½lb thin asparagus
spears, trimmed
30ml/2 tbsp raspberry vinegar
2.5ml/½ tsp salt
5ml/1 tsp Dijon mustard
25ml/1½ tbsp sunflower oil
30ml/2 tbsp sour cream
or natural (plain) yogurt
ground white pepper
175g/6oz/1 cup fresh raspberries,
to garnish

1 Fill a large frying pan with water 10cm/4in deep and bring to the boil. Tie the asparagus spears into two bundles. Cook the bundles until just tender, for about 2 minutes.

2 Remove from the pan and immerse in cold water. Drain, untie and pat dry. Chill for 1 hour.

3 Mix the vinegar, salt and mustard in a bowl. Gradually stir in the oil until it is blended. Add the sour cream or yogurt and pepper to taste.

4 To serve, place the asparagus on individual plates and drizzle the dressing across the middle of the spears. Garnish with the raspberries.

Nutritional information per portion: Energy 104kcal/431kJ; Protein 5.8g; Carbohydrate 5.8g, of which sugars 5.6g; Fat 6.5g, of which saturates 1.6g; Cholesterol 5mg; Calcium 64mg; Fibre 4g; Sodium 43mg.

Greek aubergine and spinach pie

Aubergines layered with spinach, feta cheese and rice make a flavoursome and dramatic filling for a pie. It can be served warm or cold in elegant slices.

SERVES 12

375g/13oz shortcrust pastry, thawed
   if frozen
45–60ml/3–4 tbsp olive oil
1 large aubergine (eggplant), sliced
1 onion, chopped
1 garlic clove, crushed
175g/6oz spinach, washed
4 eggs

75g/3oz/½ cup crumbled feta cheese
40g/1½oz/½ cup freshly grated
   Parmesan cheese
60ml/4 tbsp natural (plain) yogurt
90ml/6 tbsp creamy milk
225g/8oz/2 cups cooked white or brown
   long grain rice
salt and ground black pepper

1 Preheat the oven to 180°C/350°F/Gas 4. Roll out the pastry thinly and use to line a 25cm/10in flan pan. Prick the base all over and bake in the oven for 10–12 minutes until the pastry is pale golden. (Alternatively, bake blind, using baking parchment as a lining, weighted with a handful of baking beans.)

2 Heat 30–45ml/2–3 tbsp of the oil in a frying pan and fry the aubergine slices for 6–8 minutes on each side until golden. You may need to add a little more oil at first, but this will be released as the flesh softens. Lift out and drain well on kitchen paper. Add the onion and garlic to the oil remaining in the pan then fry over a gentle heat for 4–5 minutes until soft, adding a little extra oil if necessary.

3 Chop the spinach finely, by hand or in a food processor. Beat the eggs in a large mixing bowl, then add the spinach, feta, Parmesan, yogurt, milk and the onion mixture. Season well with salt and ground black pepper and stir thoroughly to mix.

4 Spread the rice in an even layer over the base of the part-baked pastry case. Reserve a few aubergine slices for the top, and arrange the rest in an even layer over the rice.

5 Spoon the spinach and feta mixture over the aubergines and place the remaining slices on top. Bake for 30–40 minutes until lightly browned. Serve the pie while warm, or leave it to cool completely before transferring to a serving plate.

Nutritional information per portion: Energy 257kcal/1075kJ; Protein 6.5g; Carbohydrate 23.8g, of which sugars 2.1g; Fat 15.8g, of which saturates 4.7g; Cholesterol 73mg; Calcium 99mg; Fibre 1.5g; Sodium 267mg.

Son-in-law eggs

The name of this recipe comes from a story about a suitor who wanted to impress his future mother-in-law and devised a recipe from the only other dish he knew how to make – boiled eggs.

SERVES 4–6

75g/3oz/generous ¹⁄₃ cup palm
    sugar (jaggery)
60ml/4 tbsp light soy sauce
105ml/7 tbsp tamarind juice
oil, for frying
6 shallots, finely sliced
6 garlic cloves, finely sliced
6 red chillies, sliced
6 hard-boiled eggs, shelled
coriander (cilantro) sprigs, to garnish
lettuce, to serve

1 Combine the palm sugar, soy sauce and tamarind juice in a small saucepan. Bring to the boil, stirring until the sugar dissolves, then simmer the sauce for about 5 minutes.

2 Taste and add more palm sugar, soy sauce or tamarind juice, if necessary. It should be sweet, salty and slightly sour. Transfer the sauce to a bowl and set aside until needed.

3 Heat a couple of spoonfuls of the oil in a frying pan and fry the shallots, garlic and chillies until golden brown. Transfer to a bowl and set aside.

4 Deep-fry the eggs in hot oil for 3–5 minutes until golden brown. Drain the eggs on kitchen paper, quarter and arrange on a bed of lettuce. Scatter the shallot mixture over, drizzle with the sauce and garnish with coriander.

Nutritional information per portion: Energy 138kcal/578kJ; Protein 6.9g; Carbohydrate 16.3g, of which sugars 15.4g; Fat 5.6g, of which saturates 1.6g; Cholesterol 190mg; Calcium 45mg; Fibre 0.5g; Sodium 547mg.

Baked Mediterranean vegetables

Crisp and golden crunchy batter surrounds these vegetables, turning them into a substantial appetizer. Make sure the fat is really hot before adding the batter or it will not rise well.

SERVES 10–12

1 small aubergine (eggplant), trimmed,
    halved and thickly sliced
1 egg
115g/4oz/1 cup plain (all-purpose) flour
300ml/¹⁄₂ pint/1¹⁄₄ cups milk
30ml/2 tbsp fresh thyme leaves,
    or 10ml/2 tsp dried
1 red onion, quartered
2 large courgettes (zucchini)
1 each red and yellow (bell) pepper,
    seeded and quartered
60–75ml/4–5 tbsp sunflower oil
salt and ground black pepper
30ml/2 tbsp freshly grated
    Parmesan cheese and fresh
    herbs, to garnish

1 Place the sliced aubergine in a colander or sieve (strainer), sprinkle generously with salt and leave for 10 minutes. Drain and pat dry on kitchen paper.

2 Meanwhile, to make the batter, beat the egg, then gradually beat in the flour and a little milk to make a smooth thick paste. Blend in the rest of the milk, add the thyme leaves and seasoning to taste and blend until smooth. Leave in a cool place until required.

3 Put the oil in a roasting pan and heat in the oven at 220°C/ 425°F/Gas 7. Add the vegetables, coat them well with the oil and return to the oven for 20 minutes until they start to cook.

4 Whisk the batter, pour over the vegetables and return to the oven for 30 minutes. If puffed up and golden, lower the heat to 190°C/ 375°F/Gas 5 for 10–15 minutes until crisp around the edges. Sprinkle with Parmesan and herbs and serve.

Nutritional information per portion: Energy 113kcal/473kJ; Protein 4.3g; Carbohydrate 11.9g, of which sugars 4.3g; Fat 5.7g, of which saturates 1.4g; Cholesterol 17mg; Calcium 89mg; Fibre 1.5g; Sodium 45mg.

Marinated feta cheese with capers

Marinating cubes of feta cheese with herbs and spices gives a marvellous flavour. This makes a delicious starter, served with hot crunchy toast.

SERVES 6

350g/12oz feta cheese
2 garlic cloves
2.5ml/¹/₂ tsp mixed peppercorns
8 coriander seeds
1 bay leaf

15–30ml/1–2 tbsp drained capers
oregano or thyme sprigs
olive oil, to cover
hot toast, kalamata olives, and chopped
    tomatoes, to serve

1 Cut the feta cheese into bitesize cubes. Thickly slice the garlic. Put the mixed peppercorns and coriander seeds in a mortar and crush lightly with a pestle.

2 Pack the feta cubes into a large preserving jar with the bay leaf, interspersing layers of cheese with garlic, crushed peppercorns and coriander, capers and the fresh oregano or thyme sprigs.

3 Pour in enough olive oil to cover the cheese. Close tightly and leave to marinate for two weeks in the fridge.

4 Lift out the feta cubes and serve on hot toast, with some chopped tomatoes, kalamata olives and a little of the flavoured oil from the jar drizzled over.

Nutritional information per portion: Energy 165kcal/683kJ; Protein 9.3g; Carbohydrate 1.3g, of which sugars 0.9g; Fat 13.6g, of which saturates 8.3g; Cholesterol 41mg; Calcium 211mg; Fibre 0.1g; Sodium 840mg.

Courgette fritters with chilli jam

Chilli jam is hot, sweet and sticky – rather like a thick chutney. It adds a delicious piquancy to these light courgette fritters, which are always a popular dish.

MAKES 12 FRITTERS

450g/1lb/3½ cups coarsely grated
  courgettes (zucchini)
50g/2oz/²⁄₃ cup freshly grated
  Parmesan cheese
2 eggs, beaten
60ml/4 tbsp plain (all-purpose) flour
vegetable oil, for frying
salt and ground black pepper

FOR THE CHILLI JAM

75ml/5 tbsp olive oil
4 large onions, diced
4 garlic cloves, chopped
1–2 green chillies, seeded and sliced
30ml/2 tbsp soft dark brown sugar

1 First make the chilli jam. Heat the oil in a pan, then add the onions and the garlic. Reduce the heat to low, then cook for 20 minutes, stirring often, until the onions are soft. Cool.

2 Transfer to a food processor or blender. Add the chillies and sugar and blend until smooth, then return the mixture to the pan. Cook for 10 minutes, stirring often, until the mixture has the consistency of jam.

3 To make the fritters, squeeze the courgettes in a dish towel, then mix with the Parmesan, eggs, flour and salt and pepper.

4 Heat enough vegetable oil to cover the base of a frying pan. Add 30ml/2 tbsp of the mixture for each fritter. Cook for 2–3 minutes on each side. Cook the rest of the fritters. Drain on kitchen paper and serve with the chilli jam.

Nutritional information per portion: Energy 157kcal/652kJ; Protein 4.4g; Carbohydrate 11.1g, of which sugars 6.1g; Fat 10.8g, of which saturates 2.2g; Cholesterol 36mg; Calcium 85mg; Fibre 1.2g; Sodium 59mg.

Sesame seed-coated falafel with tahini dip

Sesame seeds are used to give a delightfully crunchy coating to these spicy chickpea patties.
Serve with the tahini yogurt dip, and some warmed pitta bread too, if you like.

SERVES 6

250g/9oz/1¹/₃ cups dried chickpeas
2 garlic cloves, crushed
1 red chilli, seeded and finely sliced
5ml/1 tsp ground coriander
5ml/1 tsp ground cumin
15ml/1 tbsp chopped fresh mint
15ml/1 tbsp chopped fresh parsley
2 spring onions (scallions), finely chopped
1 large (US extra large) egg, beaten
sesame seeds, for coating
sunflower oil, for frying
salt and ground black pepper

FOR THE TAHINI YOGURT DIP

30ml/2 tbsp light tahini
200g/7oz/scant 1 cup natural (plain)
    live yogurt
5ml/1 tsp cayenne pepper, plus extra
    for sprinkling
15ml/1 tbsp chopped fresh mint
1 spring onion (scallion), finely sliced
fresh herbs, to garnish

1 In a bowl, cover the chickpeas with cold water and soak overnight. Drain and rinse, then place in a pan and cover with cold water. Bring to a rapid boil for 10 minutes, then simmer for 1¹/₂–2 hours.

2 Make the dip. Mix the tahini, yogurt, cayenne and mint. Sprinkle with the spring onion and extra cayenne and chill.

3 Mix the chickpeas with the garlic, chilli, spices, herbs, spring onions, seasoning and egg. Blend in a food processor until the mixture forms a coarse paste. If the paste seems too soft, chill in the fridge for 30 minutes.

4 Form the paste into 12 patties, then roll each in the sesame seeds. Fry, in batches, for 6 minutes. Serve with the dip and fresh herbs.

Nutritional information per portion: Energy 315kcal/1314kJ; Protein 14.3g; Carbohydrate 23.8g, of which sugars 3.8g; Fat 18.8g, of which saturates 2.6g; Cholesterol 32mg; Calcium 237mg; Fibre 5.8g; Sodium 63mg.

Charred artichokes with lemon oil dip

Here is a lip-smacking change from traditional fare. Artichokes are usually boiled, but dry-heat cooking also works very well. If you can get young artichokes, try roasting them over a barbecue.

SERVES 4

15ml/1 tbsp lemon juice or white
   wine vinegar
2 artichokes, trimmed
12 garlic cloves, unpeeled
90ml/6 tbsp olive oil
1 lemon
sea salt
flat leaf parsley sprigs, to garnish

1 Preheat the oven to 200°C/ 400°F/Gas 6. Add the lemon juice or vinegar to a bowl of cold water. Cut each artichoke into wedges. Pull the hairy choke out from the centre of each wedge and discard, then drop the wedges into the water.

2 Drain the wedges and place in a roasting pan with the garlic and 45ml/3 tbsp of the oil. Toss well to coat. Sprinkle with salt and roast for 40 minutes, until tender and a little charred.

3 Make the dip. Thinly pare rind from the lemon. Place the rind in a pan with water to cover. Bring to the boil, then simmer for 5 minutes. Drain, refresh in cold water, then chop.

4 Squeeze the flesh from the garlic cloves. Transfer to a bowl, mash to a paste, then add the lemon rind. Squeeze the juice from the lemon, then whisk the remaining olive oil and the lemon juice into the garlic paste. Garnish with parsley. Serve the artichokes with the lemon oil dip.

Nutritional information per portion: Energy 158kcal/651kJ; Protein 0.7g; Carbohydrate 1.3g, of which sugars 1.3g; Fat 16.7g, of which saturates 2.4g; Cholesterol 0mg; Calcium 52mg; Fibre 1.4g; Sodium 75mg.

Risotto frittata

Half omelette, half risotto, this makes a delightful appetizer. If possible, cook each frittata separately in a small, cast-iron pan, so that the eggs cook quickly but stay moist on top.

SERVES 4

30–45ml/2–3 tbsp olive oil

1 small onion, finely chopped

1 garlic clove, crushed

1 large red (bell) pepper, seeded and cut into thin strips

150g/5oz/³/4 cup risotto rice

400–475ml/14–16fl oz/1²/₃–2 cups simmering vegetable stock

25–40g/1–1¹/2 oz/2–3 tbsp butter

175g/6oz/2¹/2 cups button (white) mushrooms, finely sliced

60ml/4 tbsp freshly grated Parmesan cheese

6–8 eggs

salt and ground black pepper

1 Heat 15ml/1 tbsp oil in a frying pan and fry the onion and garlic over a gentle heat for 2–3 minutes. Add the pepper and cook, stirring, for 4–5 minutes, until soft.

2 Stir in the rice and cook gently for 2–3 minutes, stirring until the grains are evenly coated with oil.

3 Add a quarter of the vegetable stock and season. Stir over a low heat until the stock is absorbed. Add more stock, a little at a time. Let the rice absorb the liquid before adding more. Continue until the rice is al dente.

4 In a small pan, heat a little of the remaining oil and some of the butter and fry the mushrooms.

5 When the rice is tender, remove it from the heat. Stir in the mushrooms and the Parmesan.

6 Beat the eggs with 40ml/8 tsp cold water and season. Heat the remaining oil and butter in a pan and add the risotto. Spread the mixture in the pan, then add the beaten egg. Tilt the pan so that it cooks evenly. Fry over a moderate heat for 1–2 minutes, then transfer to a warmed plate and serve.

Nutritional information per portion: Energy 434kcal/1804kJ; Protein 19.5g; Carbohydrate 34.1g, of which sugars 3.6g; Fat 24.5g, of which saturates 9.5g; Cholesterol 314mg; Calcium 241mg; Fibre 1.4g; Sodium 311mg.

Wild mushroom and fontina tarts

Italian fontina cheese gives these tarts a creamy, nutty flavour. You can make the pastry cases in advance, then store in an airtight container for up to 2 days.

SERVES 4

25g/1oz/1/2 cup dried wild mushrooms
30ml/2 tbsp olive oil
1 red onion, chopped
2 garlic cloves, chopped
30ml/2 tbsp medium-dry sherry
1 egg
120ml/4fl oz/1/2 cup single (light) cream
25g/1oz fontina cheese, thinly sliced

salt and ground black pepper
rocket (arugula) leaves, to serve

FOR THE PASTRY
115g/4oz/1 cup wholemeal
  (whole-wheat) flour
50g/2oz/4 tbsp unsalted butter
25g/1oz/1/4 cup walnuts, roasted and ground
1 egg, lightly beaten

1 To make the pastry, rub the flour and butter together until the mixture resembles fine breadcrumbs. Add the nuts then the egg; mix to a soft dough. Wrap, then chill for 30 minutes.

2 Meanwhile, soak the dried wild mushrooms in 300ml/1/2 pint/11/4 cups boiling water for 30 minutes. Drain and reserve the liquid. Fry the onion in the oil for 5 minutes, then add the garlic and fry for about 2 minutes, stirring.

3 Add the soaked mushrooms and cook for 7 minutes over a high heat until the edges become crisp. Add the sherry and the reserved liquid. Cook over a high heat for about 10 minutes until the liquid evaporates. Season and set aside to cool.

4 Preheat the oven to 200°C/400°F/Gas 6. Lightly grease four 10cm/4in tart tins (muffin pans). Roll out the pastry on a lightly floured work surface and use to line the tart tins.

5 Prick the pastry, line with baking parchment and baking beans and bake blind for about 10 minutes. Remove the paper and the beans.

6 Whisk the egg and cream to mix, add to the mushroom mixture, then season. Spoon into the pastry cases, top with the cheese and bake for 18 minutes until the filling is set. Serve with rocket.

Nutritional information per portion: Energy 409kcal/1701kJ; Protein 10.2g; Carbohydrate 21.9g, of which sugars 2.3g; Fat 31g, of which saturates 13.4g; Cholesterol 143mg; Calcium 121mg; Fibre 2.3g; Sodium 199mg.

Chive scrambled eggs in brioches

This is an indulgent, truly delicious and slightly quirky start to a meal. Take care to cook the eggs at the right temperature and for the right time, otherwise they can become too dry or too sloppy.

SERVES 4

115g/4oz/¹/₂ cup unsalted butter
75g/3oz/generous 1 cup brown cap
   (cremini) mushrooms, finely sliced
4 individual brioches
8 eggs
15ml/1 tbsp chopped fresh chives, plus
   extra to garnish
salt and ground black pepper

1 Preheat the oven to 180°C/ 350°F/Gas 4. Place a quarter of the butter in a frying pan and heat until melted. Fry the mushrooms for about 3 minutes, then keep warm.

2 Slice the tops off the brioches, then scoop out the centres and discard. Put the brioches and lids on a baking sheet. Bake for 5 minutes until hot and slightly crisp.

3 Meanwhile, beat the eggs lightly and season to taste. Heat the remaining butter in a heavy pan over a gentle heat. When the butter has melted and is foaming slightly,

add the eggs. Using a wooden spoon, stir constantly to ensure the egg does not stick.

4 Continue to stir gently until about three-quarters of the egg is semi-solid and creamy – this takes 2–3 minutes. Remove the pan from the heat – the egg will continue to cook – then stir in the chives.

5 To serve, spoon a little of the mushrooms into the base of each brioche and top with the scrambled eggs. Sprinkle with extra chives, balance the brioche lids on top and serve immediately.

Nutritional information per portion: Energy 533kcal/2218kJ; Protein 17.9g; Carbohydrate 31.9g, of which sugars 9.9g; Fat 38.2g, of which saturates 19.2g; Cholesterol 443mg; Calcium 137mg; Fibre 1.7g; Sodium 507mg.

Vegetable tempura

Tempura is a Japanese type of savoury fritter. Originally prawns were used, but a variety of vegetables can be cooked in the egg batter successfully too.

SERVES 4

2 courgettes (zucchini)
¹/₂ aubergine (eggplant)
1 large carrot
¹/₂ small Spanish (Bermuda) onion
1 egg
120ml/4fl oz/¹/₂ cup iced water
115g/4oz/1 cup plain (all-purpose) flour
salt and ground black pepper
vegetable oil, for deep-frying
sea salt flakes, lemon slices and Japanese
    soy sauce, to serve

1 Pare strips of peel from the courgettes and aubergine to give a striped effect. Using a chef's knife, cut the courgettes, aubergine and carrot into strips 7.5–10cm/3–4in long and 3mm/¹/₈in wide. Place in a colander and sprinkle with salt. Weigh down with a small plate, leave for 30 minutes, then rinse. Drain then dry with kitchen paper.

2 Thinly slice the onion from top to base, discarding the middle pieces. Separate the layers to make fine, long strips. Mix all the vegetables together and season well.

3 Make the batter just before frying. Mix the egg and iced water in a bowl, then sift in the flour. Mix briefly. Do not overmix: the batter should remain lumpy. Add the vegetables to the batter and mix.

4 Half-fill a wok with oil and heat to 180°C/350°F. Carefully lower a heaped tablespoonful of the mixture at a time into the oil. Cook batches for about 3 minutes, until golden and crisp. Drain on kitchen paper.

5 Serve with salt, lemon and Japanese soy sauce for dipping.

Nutritional information per portion: Energy 313kcal/1305kJ; Protein 7.1g; Carbohydrate 30.6g, of which sugars 7.3g; Fat 18.9g, of which saturates 2.5g; Cholesterol 48mg; Calcium 94mg; Fibre 3.6g; Sodium 28mg.

Leek and onion tartlets

*Baking in individual tins makes for easier serving for a starter and it looks attractive, too.
You could make tiny tartlets for parties.*

SERVES 6

25g/1oz/2 tbsp butter
1 onion, thinly sliced
2.5ml/¹/₂ tsp dried thyme
450g/1lb leeks, thinly sliced
50g/2oz Gruyère or Emmenthal
   cheese, grated
3 eggs
300ml/¹/₂ pint/1¹/₄ cups single
   (light) cream
pinch of freshly grated nutmeg

salt and ground black pepper
mixed salad leaves, to serve

FOR THE PASTRY

175g/6oz/1¹/₃ cups plain
   (all-purpose) flour
75g/3oz/6 tbsp cold butter
1 egg yolk
30–45ml/2–3 tbsp cold water
2.5ml/¹/₂ tsp salt

1 To make the pastry, sift the flour into a bowl and add the butter. Using your fingertips, rub the butter into the flour until it resembles fine breadcrumbs. Make a well in the centre of the mixture.

2 Beat together the egg yolk, water and salt, pour into the well and combine the flour and liquid until it begins to stick together. Form into a ball. Wrap and chill for 30 minutes.

3 Butter six 10cm/4in tartlet tins (muffin pans). On a lightly floured surface, roll out the dough until 3mm/¹/₈in thick, then using a 12.5cm/5in cutter, cut as many rounds as possible. Gently ease the rounds into the tins, pressing the pastry firmly into the base and sides. Re-roll the trimmings and line the remaining tins. Prick the bases all over and chill in the fridge for 30 minutes.

4 Preheat the oven to 190°C/375°F/Gas 5. Line the pastry cases with foil and fill with baking beans. Place on a baking sheet and bake for 6–8 minutes until golden at the edges. Remove the foil and beans and bake for a further 2 minutes until the bases appear dry. Transfer to a wire rack to cool. Reduce the oven temperature to 180°C/350°F/Gas 4.

5 In a large frying pan, melt the butter over a medium heat, then add the onion and thyme and cook for 3–5 minutes until the onion is just softened, stirring frequently. Add the thinly sliced leeks and cook for 10–12 minutes until they are soft and tender, stirring occasionally. Divide the leek mixture among the pastry cases and sprinkle each with cheese, dividing it evenly.

6 In a medium bowl, beat the eggs, cream, nutmeg and salt and pepper. Place the pastry cases on a baking sheet and pour in the egg mixture. Bake for 15–20 minutes until set and golden. Transfer the tartlets to a wire rack to cool slightly, then remove them from the tins and serve warm or at room temperature with salad leaves.

Nutritional information per portion: Energy 422kcal/1755kJ; Protein 11.5g; Carbohydrate 26.8g, of which sugars 3.9g; Fat 30.4g, of which saturates 17.7g; Cholesterol 200mg; Calcium 189mg; Fibre 2.7g; Sodium 215mg.

Tortilla wrap with tabbouleh and avocado

To be successful, tabbouleh needs spring onions, lemon juice, plenty of fresh herbs and lots of black pepper. Served at room temperature, it goes very well with the chilli and avocado mixture.

SERVES 6

175g/6oz/1 cup bulgur wheat
30ml/2 tbsp chopped fresh mint
30ml/2 tbsp chopped fresh
   flat leaf parsley, plus extra to
   garnish (optional)
1 bunch (about 6) spring onions
   (scallions), sliced
1/2 cucumber, diced
50ml/2fl oz/1/4 cup extra virgin olive oil
juice of 1 large lemon
salt and freshly ground black pepper
1 ripe avocado, stoned (pitted),
   peeled and diced
juice of 1/2 lemon
1/2 red chilli, seeded and sliced
1 garlic clove, crushed
1/2 red (bell) pepper, seeded and
   finely diced
4 wheat tortillas, to serve

1 To make the tabbouleh, place the bulgur wheat in a large heatproof bowl and pour over enough boiling water to cover. Leave for 30 minutes until the grains are tender but still retain a little resistance to the bite. Drain thoroughly in a sieve, then tip back into the bowl.

2 Add the mint, parsley, spring onions and cucumber to the bulgur wheat and mix thoroughly. Blend together the olive oil and lemon juice and pour over the tabbouleh, season to taste and toss well to mix. Chill for 30 minutes to allow the flavours to mingle.

3 To make the avocado mixture, place the avocado in a bowl and add the lemon juice, chilli and garlic. Season to taste and mash with a fork to form a smooth purée. Stir in the red pepper.

4 Warm the tortillas in a dry frying pan and serve either flat, folded or rolled up with the tabbouleh and avocado mixture. Garnish with parsley, if using.

Nutritional information per portion: Energy 336kcal/1408kJ; Protein 7.2g; Carbohydrate 53.9g, of which sugars 3.3g; Fat 11.4g, of which saturates 1.9g; Cholesterol 0mg; Calcium 88mg; Fibre 3.2g; Sodium 173mg.

Mini baked potatoes with blue cheese

These miniature potatoes can be eaten with the fingers. This dish is a great way of starting off an informal supper party, but it works just as well as a light snack, using ordinary baking potatoes.

MAKES 20

20 small new or salad potatoes
60ml/4 tbsp vegetable oil
coarse salt
120ml/4fl oz/^{1}/$_2$ cup sour cream
25g/1oz blue cheese, crumbled
30ml/2 tbsp chopped fresh chives,
    to garnish

1 Preheat the oven to 180°C/350°F/Gas 4. Wash and dry the potatoes. Toss with the oil in a bowl to coat.

2 Dip the potatoes in the coarse salt to coat lightly. Spread the potatoes out on a baking sheet. Bake for 45–50 minutes until the potatoes are tender.

3 In a small bowl, combine the sour cream and blue cheese, mixing together well.

4 Cut a cross in the top of each potato. Press gently with your fingers to open the potatoes.

5 Top each potato with a dollop of the blue cheese mixture. Place on a serving dish and garnish with the chives. Serve hot or at room temperature.

Nutritional information per portion: Energy 63kcal/262kJ; Protein 1.1g; Carbohydrate 6.3g, of which sugars 0.7g; Fat 3.9g, of which saturates 1.3g; Cholesterol 5mg; Calcium 14mg; Fibre 0.4g; Sodium 22mg.

Twice-baked Gruyère and potato soufflé

A great starter dish, this recipe can be prepared in advance if you are entertaining, to be given its second baking just before you serve it up.

SERVES 4

225g/8oz floury potatoes
2 eggs, separated
175g/6oz/1½ cups Gruyère
   cheese, grated
50g/2oz/½ cup self-raising
   (self-rising) flour
50g/2oz spinach leaves
butter, for greasing
salt and ground black pepper
salad leaves, to serve

1 Preheat the oven to 200°C/400°F/Gas 6. Peel the potatoes and cook in lightly salted boiling water for 20 minutes until very tender. Drain and mash with the egg yolks.

2 Stir in half of the Gruyère cheese and all of the flour. Season to taste with salt and ground black pepper. Finely chop the spinach and fold into the potato mixture.

3 Whip the egg whites until they form soft peaks. Fold a little of the egg white into the mixture to slacken it slightly. Using a large spoon, fold the remaining egg white into the mixture.

4 Grease 4 large ramekin dishes. Pour the mixture into the dishes; place on a baking sheet. Bake for 20 minutes. Remove from the oven and allow to cool.

5 Turn the soufflés out on to a baking sheet and scatter with the remaining cheese. Bake again for 5 minutes; serve with salad leaves.

Nutritional information per portion: Energy 304kcal/1270kJ; Protein 16.7g; Carbohydrate 19g, of which sugars 1.2g; Fat 17.5g, of which saturates 10.4g; Cholesterol 138mg; Calcium 380mg; Fibre 1.2g; Sodium 376mg.

Fried rice balls stuffed with mozzarella

These deep-fried balls of risotto go by the name of suppli al telefono *in their native Italy. Stuffed with mozzarella cheese, they are very popular snacks and make a wonderful start to any meal.*

SERVES 4

1 quantity Risotto alla Milanese, made
   without the saffron and with
   vegetable stock (see page 181)
3 eggs
breadcrumbs and plain (all-purpose)
   flour, to coat
115g/4oz/²/₃ cup mozzarella cheese, cut
   into small cubes
oil, for deep-frying
dressed frisée lettuce and cherry
   tomatoes, to serve

1 Put the risotto in a bowl and allow it to cool completely. Beat two of the eggs, and stir them into the cooled risotto until well mixed.

2 Use your hands to form the rice mixture into balls the size of large eggs. If the mixture is too moist to hold its shape well, stir in a few spoonfuls of breadcrumbs. Poke a hole in the centre of each ball with your finger, then fill it with the mozzarella, and close the hole over again with the rice mixture.

3 Heat the oil for deep-frying until a small piece of bread sizzles as soon as it is dropped in.

4 Spread some flour on a plate. Beat the remaining egg in a shallow bowl. Sprinkle another plate with breadcrumbs. Roll the balls in the flour, then in the egg, and finally in the breadcrumbs. Fry the rice balls, a few at a time, in the hot oil until golden and crisp. Drain on kitchen paper while the remaining balls are being fried and keep warm. Serve at once, with a simple salad of frisée lettuce and cherry tomatoes.

Nutritional information per portion: Energy 813kcal/3389kJ; Protein 28.9g; Carbohydrate 89.6g, of which sugars 1.9g; Fat 37.9g, of which saturates 22.1g; Cholesterol 233mg; Calcium 464mg; Fibre 0.8g; Sodium 754mg.

Vegetable tarte tatin

This upside-down tart combines Mediterranean vegetables with rice, garlic, onions and olives. Courgettes and mushrooms could be used as well.

SERVES 4

30ml/2 tbsp sunflower oil

about 25ml/1¹/₂ tbsp olive oil

1 aubergine (eggplant), sliced lengthways

1 large red (bell) pepper, seeded and cut into
   long strips

5 tomatoes

2 red shallots, finely chopped

1–2 garlic cloves, crushed

150ml/¹/₄ pint/²/₃ cup white wine

10ml/2 tsp chopped fresh basil

225g/8oz/2 cups cooked white or brown long grain rice

40g/1¹/₂oz/²/₃ cup stoned (pitted) black
   olives, chopped

350g/12oz puff pastry, thawed if frozen

ground black pepper

salad leaves, to serve

1 Preheat the oven to 190°C/375°F/Gas 5. Heat the sunflower oil with 15ml/1 tbsp of the olive oil and fry the aubergine slices for 4–5 minutes on each side. Drain on kitchen paper.

2 Add the pepper strips to the oil in the pan, turning them to coat. Cover the pan with a lid or foil and sweat the peppers over a moderately high heat for 5–6 minutes, stirring occasionally, until they are soft and flecked with brown.

3 Slice two of the tomatoes and set them aside. Plunge the remaining tomatoes briefly into boiling water, then peel them, cut them into quarters and remove the core and seeds. Chop the tomato flesh roughly.

4 Heat the remaining oil in the pan and fry the shallots and garlic for 3–4 minutes until softened. Add the chopped tomatoes and cook for a few minutes until softened. Stir in the wine and basil, with black pepper. Bring to the boil, then remove from the heat and stir in the rice and olives.

5 Arrange the tomato slices, aubergine slices and peppers in a single layer on the base of a heavy, 30cm/12in, shallow ovenproof dish. Spread the rice mixture on top.

6 Roll out the pastry to a circle slightly larger than the diameter of the dish and place on top of the rice, tucking the overlap down inside the dish. Bake for 25–30 minutes, until the pastry is golden. Cool slightly, then invert the tart on to a warmed serving plate. Serve in slices, with salad leaves.

Nutritional information per portion: Energy 535kcal/2240kJ; Protein 8.2g; Carbohydrate 59.1g, of which sugars 8.8g; Fat 29.5g, of which saturates 1.2g; Cholesterol 0mg; Calcium 89mg; Fibre 2.6g; Sodium 521mg.

Buckwheat blinis with mushroom caviar

These little Russian pancakes are traditionally served with fish roe caviar and sour cream. Here is a vegetarian alternative that uses a selection of delicious wild mushrooms in place of fish roe.

SERVES 4

115g/4oz/1 cup strong white bread flour
50g/2oz/¹/₂ cup buckwheat flour
2.5ml/¹/₂ tsp salt
300ml/¹/₂ pint/1¹/₄ cups milk
5ml/1 tsp dried yeast
2 eggs, separated
200ml/7fl oz/scant 1 cup sour cream
    or crème fraîche

FOR THE CAVIAR

350g/12oz mixed wild mushrooms,
    such as chanterelle and porcini,
    trimmed and chopped
5ml/1 tsp celery salt
30ml/2 tbsp walnut oil
15ml/1 tbsp lemon juice
45ml/3 tbsp chopped fresh parsley
ground black pepper

1 To make the caviar, place the mushrooms in a glass bowl, toss with the salt and cover with a weighted plate. Leave for 2 hours until the juices have run out into the base of the bowl. Rinse to remove the salt, drain and press out as much liquid as you can with the back of a spoon. Return the mushrooms to the bowl and toss with walnut oil, lemon juice, parsley and pepper. Chill.

2 Sift the two flours together with the salt in a large mixing bowl. Gently warm the milk then add the yeast, stirring until dissolved. Pour into the flour, add the egg yolks and stir to make a smooth batter. Cover with a clean damp dish towel and leave in a warm place for 1 hour.

3 Whisk the egg whites in a clean grease-free bowl until stiff then fold into the risen batter. Heat an iron pan or griddle to a moderate temperature. Moisten with oil, then drop spoonfuls of the batter on to the surface. When bubbles rise to the top, turn them over and cook briefly on the other side. Spoon on the sour cream or crème fraîche, top with the caviar and serve.

Nutritional information per portion: Energy 380kcal/1586kJ; Protein 12.5g; Carbohydrate 38.8g, of which sugars 6.2g; Fat 20.6g, of which saturates 8.5g; Cholesterol 130mg; Calcium 205mg; Fibre 2.3g; Sodium 94mg.

Pears and Stilton

Stilton is the classic British blue cheese, but you could use other blue cheeses. Comice pears are a good choice for this dish, but for a dramatic colour contrast, select the excellent Red Williams.

SERVES 4

4 ripe pears, lightly chilled
75g/3oz blue Stilton
50g/2oz curd (farmer's) cheese
ground black pepper
watercress sprigs, to garnish

FOR THE DRESSING

45ml/3 tbsp light olive oil
15ml/1 tbsp lemon juice
10ml/2 tsp toasted poppy seeds
salt and ground black pepper

1 First make the dressing: place the olive oil and lemon juice, poppy seeds and seasoning in a screw-top jar and then shake together until emulsified.

2 Cut the pears in half lengthways, then scoop out the cores and cut away the calyx from the rounded end.

3 Beat together the Stilton, curd cheese and a little pepper. Divide this mixture among the cavities in the pears.

4 Shake the dressing to mix it again, then spoon it over the pears. Serve garnished with some watercress sprigs.

Nutritional information per portion: Energy 243kcal/1007kJ; Protein 7.2g; Carbohydrate 15.5g, of which sugars 15.5g; Fat 17.2g, of which saturates 6.4g; Cholesterol 21mg; Calcium 109mg; Fibre 3.5g; Sodium 208mg.

Fish and shellfish

Fish lends itself perfectly to appetizers because it is so versatile. In these recipes, fish is turned into sausages, kebabs, batons and delicious puff parcels. Easy-to-cook shellfish forms the basis for some of the great classic starters such as Marinated Mussels and Crab Cakes with Tartare Sauce.

Three-colour fish kebabs

Don't leave the fish to marinate for more than an hour. The lemon juice will start to break down the fibres of the fish after this time and it will then be difficult to avoid overcooking it.

SERVES 4

120ml/4fl oz/½ cup olive oil
grated rind and juice of 1 lemon
5ml/1 tsp crushed chilli flakes
350g/12oz monkfish fillet, cubed
350g/12oz swordfish fillet, cubed
350g/12oz thick salmon fillet, cubed
2 red, yellow or orange (bell) peppers,
    cored, seeded and cut into squares
30ml/2 tbsp chopped fresh parsley
salt and ground black pepper

FOR THE SWEET TOMATO AND CHILLI SALSA

225g/8oz ripe tomatoes, finely chopped
1 garlic clove, crushed
1 fresh red chilli, seeded and chopped
45ml/3 tbsp extra virgin olive oil
15ml/1 tbsp lemon juice
15ml/1 tbsp chopped fresh parsley
pinch of sugar

1 Put the oil in a shallow glass or china bowl and add the lemon rind and juice, the chilli flakes and pepper to taste. Whisk to combine, then add the fish chunks. Turn to coat evenly.

2 Add the pepper squares, stir, then cover and marinate in a cool place for 1 hour, turning occasionally with a slotted spoon.

3 Thread the fish and peppers on to eight oiled metal skewers, reserving the marinade. Barbecue or grill (broil) the skewered fish for 5–8 minutes, turning once.

4 Meanwhile, make the salsa by mixing all the ingredients in a bowl, and then add seasoning to taste. Heat the reserved marinade in a small pan, remove from the heat and stir in the parsley, with salt and pepper to taste. Serve the kebabs hot, with the marinade spooned over, accompanied by the salsa.

Nutritional information per portion: Energy 506kcal/2108kJ; Protein 37.4g; Carbohydrate 14.4g, of which sugars 0.6g; Fat 33.6g, of which saturates 13.7g; Cholesterol 130mg; Calcium 75mg; Fibre 0.6g; Sodium 1414mg.

Breaded sole batons

Goujons of lemon sole are coated in seasoned flour and then in breadcrumbs, and fried until deliciously crispy. They are served with piquant tartare sauce.

SERVES 4

275g/10oz lemon sole fillets, skinned
2 eggs
115g/4oz/1¹/₂ cups fine
   fresh breadcrumbs
75g/3oz/6 tbsp plain (all-purpose) flour
salt and ground black pepper
vegetable oil, for frying
tartare sauce and lemon wedges,
   to serve

1 Cut the fish fillets into long diagonal strips about 2cm/³⁄₄in wide, using a sharp knife.

2 Break the eggs into a shallow dish and beat well with a fork. Place the breadcrumbs in another shallow dish. Put the flour in a large plastic bag and season with salt and plenty of ground black pepper.

3 Dip the fish strips in the egg, turning to coat well. Place on a plate and then taking a few at a time, shake them in the bag of flour. Dip the strips in the egg again, then in the breadcrumbs, coating well. Place on a tray in a single layer. Let the coating set for 10 minutes.

4 Heat 1cm/¹/₂in oil in a large frying pan over a medium-high heat. When the oil is hot (a cube of bread will sizzle) fry the fish strips for about 2–2¹/₂ minutes in batches, turning once. Drain on kitchen paper and keep warm. Serve the fish with tartare sauce and lemon wedges.

Nutritional information per portion: Energy 363kcal/1522kJ; Protein 20.7g; Carbohydrate 36.9g, of which sugars 1g; Fat 15.8g, of which saturates 2.1g; Cholesterol 130mg; Calcium 98mg; Fibre 1.2g; Sodium 323mg.

Fish sausages

This unusual recipe originated in Hungary during the seventeenth century. It is still popular today as a satisfying and tasty way of using a variety of fish fillets.

SERVES 4

375g/13oz fish fillets, such as perch,
   pike, carp or cod, skinned
1 white bread roll
75ml/5 tbsp milk
25ml/1½ tbsp chopped fresh flat
   leaf parsley
2 eggs, well beaten
50g/2oz/½ cup plain (all-purpose) flour
50g/2oz/1 cup fine fresh
   white breadcrumbs
oil, for shallow frying
salt and ground black pepper
deep-fried parsley sprigs and lemon
   wedges dusted with paprika,
     to garnish

1 Mince or process the fish coarsely in a food processor or blender. Soak the roll in the milk for about 10 minutes, then squeeze it out. Mix the fish and bread together before adding the chopped parsley, one of the eggs and plenty of seasoning.

2 Using your fingers, shape the fish mixture into 10cm/4in long sausages, making them about 2.5cm/1in thick. Carefully roll the fish "sausages" in the flour, then in the remaining egg and finally in the breadcrumbs.

3 Heat the oil in a pan then slowly cook the sausages until golden brown all over. (You may need to work in batches.) Drain well on crumpled kitchen paper. Garnish with the deep-fried parsley sprigs and lemon wedges dusted with paprika.

Nutritional information per portion: Energy 238kcal/1007kJ; Protein 24.7g; Carbohydrate 25.8g, of which sugars 1.7g; Fat 4.8g, of which saturates 1.4g; Cholesterol 139mg; Calcium 82mg; Fibre 1.2g; Sodium 292mg.

Deep-fried whitebait

A spicy coating on these fish, which is a mixture of ground ginger, curry powder and cayenne pepper, gives this ever popular dish a crunchy bite.

SERVES 6

115g/4oz/1 cup plain (all-purpose) flour
2.5ml/¹/₂ tsp curry powder
2.5ml/¹/₂ tsp ground ginger
2.5ml/¹/₂ tsp cayenne pepper
pinch of salt
1.2kg/2¹/₂ lb whitebait, thawed if frozen
vegetable oil, for deep-frying
lemon wedges, to garnish

1 Mix together the plain flour, curry powder, ground ginger, cayenne pepper and a little salt in a large bowl. Coat the fish in the seasoned flour, covering them evenly.

2 Heat the oil in a large, heavy pan until it reaches a temperature of 190°C/375°F. Fry the whitebait in batches for about 2–3 minutes until the fish is golden and crispy.

3 Drain the whitebait well on kitchen paper. Keep warm in a low oven until you have cooked all the fish. Serve at once, garnished with lemon wedges for squeezing over.

Nutritional information per portion: Energy 1050kcal/4348kJ; Protein 39g; Carbohydrate 10.6g, of which sugars 0.2g; Fat 95g, of which saturates 0g; Cholesterol 0mg; Calcium 1720mg; Fibre 0.4g; Sodium 460mg.

Herby plaice fritters

Serve these baby croquettes with a tartare sauce if you like, or use a good-quality mayonnaise and stir in some chopped capers and gherkins. Season to taste.

SERVES 4

450g/1lb plaice fillets
300ml/¹/₂ pint/1¹/₄ cups milk
450g/1lb cooked potatoes
1 fennel bulb, finely chopped
45ml/ 3 tbsp chopped fresh parsley
2 eggs
15g/¹/₂ oz/1 tbsp unsalted butter
250g/9oz/2 cups white breadcrumbs
25g/1oz/2 tbsp sesame seeds
oil, for deep-frying
salt and ground black pepper

1 Gently poach the plaice fillets in the milk for about 15 minutes until the fish flakes. Drain and reserve the milk. Peel the skin off the fish and remove any bones. In a food processor fitted with a metal blade, process the fish, potatoes, fennel, parsley, eggs and butter.

2 Add 30ml/2 tbsp of the reserved cooking milk and season. Mix well. Chill for 30 minutes then shape into 20 even-size croquettes.

3 Mix together the breadcrumbs and sesame seeds, then roll the croquettes in this mixture to form a good coating.

4 Heat the oil in a large, heavy pan until it is hot enough to brown a cube of stale bread in 30 seconds. Deep-fry the croquettes in small batches for about 4 minutes until they are golden brown all over. Drain well on kitchen paper and serve the fritters hot.

Nutritional information per portion: Energy 596kcal/2510kJ; Protein 32.7g; Carbohydrate 67.5g, of which sugars 4g; Fat 23.7g, of which saturates 4.9g; Cholesterol 150mg; Calcium 208mg; Fibre 4.2g; Sodium 687mg.

Paella croquettes

Paella is probably Spain's most famous dish, and here it is used for a tasty fried tapas. In this recipe, the paella is cooked from scratch, but you could, of course, use left-over paella instead.

SERVES 4

pinch of saffron threads
150ml/¼ pint/⅔ cup white wine
30ml/2 tbsp olive oil
1 small onion, finely chopped
1 garlic clove, finely chopped
150g/5oz/⅔ cup risotto rice
300ml/½ pint/1¼ cups hot
　chicken stock
50g/2oz/1½ cup cooked prawns (shrimp),
　peeled, deveined and coarsely chopped
50g/2oz cooked chicken, chopped
75g/3oz/⅔ cup petits pois, thawed
　if frozen
30ml/2 tbsp grated Parmesan cheese
1 egg, beaten
30ml/2 tbsp milk
75g/3oz/1½ cups fresh
　white breadcrumbs
vegetable or olive oil, for shallow-frying
salt and ground black pepper
flat leaf parsley, to garnish

1 Stir the saffron into the wine in a small bowl; set aside.

2 Heat the oil in a saucepan and gently fry the onion and garlic for 5 minutes until soft. Stir in the rice and cook, stirring, for 1 minute. Keeping the heat fairly high, add the wine and saffron mixture to the pan, stirring until it is all absorbed.

3 Gradually add the stock, stirring until the liquid is absorbed and the rice is cooked – about 20 minutes. Stir in the prawns, chicken, petits pois and Parmesan cheese. Season.

4 Cool the mixture slightly, then use spoons to shape the mixture into 16 lozenges.

5 Mix the egg and milk in a shallow bowl. Spread out the breadcrumbs on a sheet of foil. Dip the croquettes in the egg mixture, then coat them evenly in the breadcrumbs.

6 Heat the oil in a frying pan, then shallow fry the croquettes for 4–5 minutes until crisp and golden. Work in batches. Drain on kitchen paper and keep hot. Serve garnished with a sprig of flat leaf parsley.

Nutritional information per portion: Energy 524kcal/2183kJ; Protein 16.2g; Carbohydrate 48.4g, of which sugars 2.3g; Fat 27.3g, of which saturates 4.9g; Cholesterol 85mg; Calcium 160mg; Fibre 1.5g; Sodium 280mg.

Monkfish packages

With its meaty flesh and robust flavour, monkfish is perfect with garlic and chilli in this recipe. You could use a cheaper fish, like eel, but you'll lose that delicious taste.

SERVES 4

175g/6oz/1¹/₂ cups strong white
    bread flour
2 eggs
115g/4oz skinless monkfish fillet, diced
grated rind of 1 lemon
1 garlic clove, chopped
1 small red chilli, seeded and sliced
45ml/3 tbsp chopped fresh parsley
30ml/2 tbsp single (light) cream
salt and ground black pepper

FOR THE TOMATO OIL

2 tomatoes, peeled, seeded and
    finely diced
45ml/3 tbsp extra virgin olive oil
15ml/1 tbsp lemon juice

1 Place the bread flour, eggs and 2.5ml/¹/₂ tsp salt in a blender or food processor; pulse until it forms a soft dough. Knead for 2–3 minutes. Wrap in clear film and chill for 20 minutes. Clean the food processor.

2 Place the monkfish, lemon rind, garlic, chilli and parsley in the food processor; process until very finely chopped. Add the cream, with plenty of salt and ground black pepper, and process again until a very thick paste is formed. Make the tomato oil by stirring the diced tomatoes with the olive oil and lemon juice in a bowl. Add salt to taste. Cover and chill.

3 Roll out the dough thinly on a lightly floured surface and cut out 32 rounds, using a 4cm/1¹/₂in plain cutter. Divide the filling among half the rounds, then cover with the remaining rounds. Pinch the edges to seal.

4 Bring a pan of water to a simmer and poach the fish packages in batches, for 2–3 minutes. Drain and serve hot, drizzled with the tomato oil.

Nutritional information per portion: Energy 310kcal/1304kJ; Protein 12.9g; Carbohydrate 36.8g, of which sugars 3.4g; Fat 13.5g, of which saturates 3.1g; Cholesterol 103mg; Calcium 112mg; Fibre 2.7g; Sodium 54mg.

Salmon cakes with butter sauce

Salmon fish cakes make a real treat for the start of a dinner party. They are also economical, as you could use any small tail pieces that are on offer from your fishmonger or supermarket.

MAKES 6

225g/8oz salmon tail piece, cooked
30ml/2 tbsp chopped fresh parsley
2 spring onions (scallions), trimmed
    and chopped
grated rind and juice of ¹/₂ lemon
225g/8oz mashed potato (not too soft)
1 egg, beaten
50g/2oz/1 cup fresh white breadcrumbs
75g/3oz/6 tbsp butter, plus extra for
    frying (optional)
oil, for frying (optional)
salt and ground black pepper
courgette (zucchini) and carrot slices and
    sprig of coriander (cilantro), to garnish

1 Remove all the skin and bones from the fish and mash or flake it well. Add the parsley, spring onions and 5ml/1 tsp of the lemon rind, and season with salt and lots of black pepper. Gently work in the potato and then shape into six rounds, triangles or croquettes. Chill the salmon cakes for 20 minutes.

2 Preheat the grill (broiler). Coat the salmon cakes well in egg and then in the breadcrumbs. Grill (broil) gently for 5 minutes on each side, or until they are golden, or fry in butter and oil.

3 To make the butter sauce, melt the butter, whisk in the remaining lemon rind, the lemon juice, 15–30ml/1–2 tbsp water and seasoning to taste. Simmer for a few minutes and serve with the hot fish cakes and garnish with slices of courgette and carrot and a sprig of coriander.

Nutritional information per portion: Energy 188kcal/782kJ; Protein 9.5g; Carbohydrate 6.2g, of which sugars 0.7g; Fat 14.1g, of which saturates 6.8g; Cholesterol 68mg; Calcium 36mg; Fibre 0.9g; Sodium 101mg.

Thai fish cakes with cucumber relish

These wonderful small fish cakes are a very familiar and popular starter. They are usually accompanied with Thai beer – or choose a robust oaked Chardonnay instead.

MAKES ABOUT 12

300g/11oz white fish fillet, such as cod,
   cut into chunks
30ml/2 tbsp red curry paste
1 egg
30ml/2 tbsp fish sauce
5ml/1 tsp sugar
30ml/2 tbsp cornflour (cornstarch)
3 kaffir lime leaves, shredded
15ml/1 tbsp chopped fresh coriander
   (cilantro)
50g/2oz green beans, finely sliced
oil, for frying
Chinese mustard cress, to garnish

FOR THE CUCUMBER RELISH
60ml/4 tbsp Thai coconut or rice vinegar
60ml/4 tbsp water
50g/2oz sugar
1 whole bulb pickled garlic
1 cucumber, quartered and sliced
4 shallots, finely sliced
15ml/1 tbsp chopped fresh root ginger

1 To make the cucumber relish, bring the vinegar, water and sugar to the boil. Stir until the sugar dissolves, then remove from the heat and leave to cool.

2 Combine the rest of the relish ingredients together in a bowl and pour the vinegar mixture over.

3 Combine the fish, curry paste and egg in a food processor and process well. Transfer the mixture to a bowl then add the rest of the ingredients, except the oil and garnish. Stir to mix thoroughly.

4 Mould and shape the mixture into cakes about 5cm/2in in diameter and 5mm/¼in thick.

5 Heat the oil in a wok or deep-fryer. Fry the fish cakes, working in small batches, for about 4–5 minutes or until golden brown. Remove and drain on kitchen paper. Keep warm in a low oven. Garnish with Chinese mustard cress and serve with a little cucumber relish spooned on the side.

Nutritional information per portion: Energy 86kcal/361kJ; Protein 6.2g; Carbohydrate 8.1g, of which sugars 5.4g; Fat 3.4g, of which saturates 0.5g; Cholesterol 27mg; Calcium 16mg; Fibre 0.2g; Sodium 2040mg.

Marinated mussels

This is an ideal recipe to prepare and arrange up to 24 hours in advance. Remove from the fridge 15 minutes before serving to allow the flavours to develop fully.

MAKES ABOUT 48

1kg/2¼lb mussels, large if possible
   (about 48)
175ml/6fl oz/¾ cup dry white wine
1 garlic clove, finely crushed
120ml/4fl oz/½ cup olive oil
50ml/2fl oz/¼ cup lemon juice
5ml/1 tsp hot chilli flakes
2.5ml/½ tsp mixed (apple pie) spice
15ml/1 tbsp Dijon mustard

10ml/2 tsp sugar
5ml/1 tsp salt
15–30ml/1–2 tbsp chopped fresh dill
   or coriander (cilantro)
15ml/1 tbsp capers, drained and chopped
   if large
ground black pepper

1 With a stiff kitchen brush and under cold running water, scrub the mussels to remove any sand and barnacles; pull out and remove the "beards". Discard any open shells that will not shut when they are tapped.

2 In a large casserole or pan set over a high heat, bring the white wine to the boil with the garlic and freshly ground black pepper. Add the mussels and cover. Reduce the heat to medium and simmer for 2–4 minutes until the shells open, stirring occasionally.

3 In a large bowl combine the olive oil, lemon juice, chilli flakes, mixed spice, Dijon mustard, sugar, salt, the chopped dill or coriander and the capers. Stir well then set aside.

4 Discard any mussels with closed shells. With a small sharp knife, carefully remove the remaining mussels from their shells, reserving the half shells for serving. Add the mussels to the marinade. Toss the mussels to coat well, then cover and chill in the fridge for 6–8 hours or overnight, stirring gently from time to time.

5 With a teaspoon, place one mussel with a little marinade in each shell and arrange on a platter. To stop them wobbling, they can be placed on crushed ice, well washed seaweed or coarse salt.

Nutritional information per portion: Energy 21kcal/86kJ; Protein 1.1g; Carbohydrate 0.3g, of which sugars 0.3g; Fat 1.4g, of which saturates 0.2g; Cholesterol 3mg; Calcium 15mg; Fibre 0.1g; Sodium 23mg.

Thai-style seafood turnovers

These elegant appetizer-size turnovers are filled with fish, prawns and Thai fragrant rice, and are subtly flavoured with fresh coriander, garlic and ginger.

MAKES 18

plain (all-purpose) flour, for dusting
500g/1¼lb puff pastry, thawed if frozen
1 egg, beaten with 30ml/2 tbsp water
lime twists, to garnish

FOR THE FILLING
275g/10oz skinned white fish fillets,
   such as cod or haddock
seasoned plain (all-purpose) flour
8–10 large raw prawns (shrimp)
15ml/1 tbsp sunflower oil

about 75g/3oz/6 tbsp butter
6 spring onions (scallions), finely sliced
1 garlic clove, crushed
225g/8oz/2 cups cooked Thai
   fragrant rice
4cm/1½ in piece fresh root
   ginger, grated
10ml/2 tsp finely chopped
   fresh coriander (cilantro)
5ml/1 tsp finely grated lime rind

1 Preheat the oven to 190°C/375°F/Gas 5. Make the filling. Cut the fish into 2cm/¾in cubes and dust with seasoned flour. Peel the prawns, remove the veins and cut each one into four pieces.

2 Heat half of the oil and 15g/½oz/1 tbsp of the butter in a frying pan. Fry the spring onions gently for 2 minutes.

3 Add the garlic and fry for a further 5 minutes, until the onions are very soft. Transfer to a large bowl.

4 Heat the remaining oil and a further 25g/1oz/2 tbsp of the butter in a clean pan. Fry the fish pieces briefly. As soon as they begin to turn opaque, use a slotted spoon to transfer them to the bowl with the spring onions. Cook the prawns in the fat remaining in the pan. When they begin to change colour, lift them out and add them to the bowl.

5 Add the cooked rice to the bowl, with the fresh root ginger, coriander and grated lime rind. Mix, taking care not to break up the fish.

6 Dust the work surface with a little flour. Roll out the pastry and cut into 10cm/4in rounds. Place spoonfuls of filling just off centre on the pastry rounds. Dot with a little of the remaining butter. Dampen the edges of the pastry with a little of the egg wash, fold one side of the pastry over the filling and press the edges together firmly.

7 Place the turnovers on two lightly greased baking sheets. Decorate them with the pastry trimmings, if you like, and brush them with egg wash. Bake in the oven for 12–15 minutes or until golden brown all over. Transfer to a plate and garnish with lime twists.

Nutritional information per portion: Energy 171kcal/715kJ; Protein 8.6g; Carbohydrate 18.7g, of which sugars 0.9g; Fat 7g, of which saturates 2.3g; Cholesterol 48mg; Calcium 34mg; Fibre 0.4g; Sodium 99mg.

Spinach empanadillas

These are little pastry turnovers, filled with ingredients that have a strong Moorish influence – pine nuts and raisins. Serve with pre-dinner drinks at an informal supper party.

MAKES 20

25g/1oz/2 tbsp raisins, soaked
25ml/1¹⁄₂ tbsp olive oil
450g/1lb fresh spinach, washed
  and chopped
6 drained canned anchovies, chopped
2 garlic cloves, finely chopped
25g/1oz/¹⁄₃ cup pine nuts, chopped
1 egg, beaten
350g/12oz puff pastry
salt and ground black pepper

1 Drain the raisins then chop roughly. Heat the oil in a pan, add the spinach, stir, cover and cook over a low heat for 2 minutes. Uncover and turn up the heat to evaporate any liquid. Add the anchovies, garlic and seasoning. Cook, stirring, for a further minute. Remove from the heat, add the raisins and pine nuts, and cool.

2 Preheat the oven to 180°C/350°F/Gas 4. Roll out the pastry to a 3mm/¹⁄₈in thickness. Using a 7.5cm/3in pastry cutter, cut out 20 rounds. Re-roll if necessary. Place two teaspoonfuls of the filling in the middle of each round, then brush the edges with water. Bring up the sides of the pastry and seal well.

3 Press the edges of the pastry together with a fork. Brush with egg. Place on a lightly greased baking sheet and bake for 15 minutes, until golden. Serve warm.

Nutritional information per portion: Energy 98kcal/409kJ; Protein 2.5g; Carbohydrate 8.6g, of which sugars 1.9g; Fat 6g, of which saturates 0.6g; Cholesterol 14mg; Calcium 29mg; Fibre 0.2g; Sodium 92mg.

Crab and ricotta tartlets

Use the meat from a freshly cooked crab, weighing about 450g/1lb, if you can. Otherwise, look out for frozen brown and white crab meat as an alternative.

SERVES 4

225g/8oz/2 cups plain (all-purpose) flour
pinch of salt
115g/4oz/1/2 cup butter, diced
225g/8oz/1 cup ricotta cheese
15ml/1 tbsp grated onion
30ml/2 tbsp grated Parmesan cheese
2.5ml/1/2 tsp mustard powder
2 eggs, plus 1 egg yolk
225g/8oz crab meat
30ml/2 tbsp chopped fresh parsley
2.5–5ml/1/2–1 tsp anchovy essence
5–10ml/1–2 tsp lemon juice
salt and cayenne pepper
salad leaves, to garnish

1 Preheat the oven to 200°C/400°F/ Gas 6. Sift the flour and salt into a bowl, add the butter and rub it in until it resembles fine breadcrumbs. Stir in about 60ml/4 tbsp cold water.

2 Turn the dough on to a floured surface and knead lightly. Roll out and line four 10cm/4in tartlet tins (muffin pans). Prick the bases with a fork, then chill for 30 minutes.

3 Line with baking parchment and fill with baking beans. Bake for 10 minutes, remove the paper and beans and bake for 10 minutes.

4 Place the ricotta, onion, Parmesan and mustard powder in a bowl and beat until soft. Gradually beat in the eggs and egg yolk.

5 Stir in the crab meat and chopped fresh parsley, then add the anchovy essence and lemon juice. Season to taste with salt and cayenne pepper.

6 Remove the tartlet cases from the oven and reduce the temperature to 180°C/350°F/Gas 4. Spoon the filling into the cases and bake for 20 minutes, until set and golden. Serve hot, garnished with salad leaves.

Nutritional information per portion: Energy 644kcal/2685kJ; Protein 28.1g; Carbohydrate 46.3g, of which sugars 3.3g; Fat 39.8g, of which saturates 23g; Cholesterol 278mg; Calcium 288mg; Fibre 2.4g; Sodium 609mg.

Seafood pancakes

The combination of fresh and smoked haddock imparts a wonderful flavour to the filling. Using pancakes makes this a substantial starter for a dinner party.

SERVES 6

FOR THE PANCAKES
115g/4oz/1 cup plain (all-purpose) flour
pinch of salt
1 egg, plus 1 egg yolk
300ml/1/2 pint/11/4 cups milk
15ml/1 tbsp melted butter, plus extra
    for cooking
50–75g/2–3oz Gruyère cheese, grated
frisée lettuce, to serve

FOR THE FILLING
225g/8oz smoked haddock fillet
225g/8oz fresh haddock fillet
300ml/1/2 pint/11/4 cups milk
150ml/1/4 pint/2/3 cup single
    (light) cream
40g/11/2 oz/3 tbsp butter
40g/11/2 oz/1/4 cup plain
    (all-purpose) flour
freshly grated nutmeg
2 hard-boiled eggs, peeled and chopped

1 To make the pancakes, sift the flour and salt into a bowl. Make a well in the centre and add the egg and extra yolk. Whisk the egg, starting to incorporate some of the flour.

2 Gradually add the milk, whisking all the time until the batter is smooth and has the consistency of thin cream. Stir in the melted butter.

3 Heat a small crêpe pan or omelette pan until hot, then rub round the inside of the pan with a pad of kitchen paper dipped in melted butter.

4 Pour about 30ml/2 tbsp of the batter into the pan, then tip the pan to coat the base evenly. Cook for about 30 seconds until the underside of the pancake is brown.

5 Flip the pancake over and cook on the other side until it is lightly browned. Repeat to make 12 pancakes, rubbing the pan with melted butter between each pancake. Stack the pancakes as you make them, between sheets of baking parchment. Keep the pancakes warm on a plate that is set over a pan of simmering water.

6 Put the haddock fillets in a large pan. Add the milk and poach for 6–8 minutes, until just tender. Lift out the fish using a slotted spoon and, when cool enough to handle, remove the skin and any bones. Reserve the milk.

7 Measure the single cream into a jug then strain enough of the milk into the jug to make the quantity up to 450ml/¾ pint/scant 2 cups in total.

8 Melt the butter in a pan, stir in the flour and cook gently for 1 minute. Gradually mix in the milk mixture, stirring continuously to make a smooth sauce. Cook for 2–3 minutes, until thickened. Season with salt, black pepper and nutmeg. Roughly flake the haddock and fold into the sauce with the eggs. Leave to cool.

9 Preheat the oven to 180°C/350°F/Gas 4. Divide the filling among the pancakes. Fold the sides of each pancake into the centre, then roll them up to enclose the filling completely.

10 Butter six individual ovenproof dishes and then arrange two filled pancakes in each, or butter one large dish for all the pancakes. Brush with melted butter and cook for 15 minutes. Sprinkle over the Gruyère and cook for a further 5 minutes, until warmed through. Serve hot with lettuce leaves.

Nutritional information per portion: Energy 393kcal/1647kJ; Protein 26.7g; Carbohydrate 25.4g, of which sugars 5.7g; Fat 21.2g, of which saturates 11.9g; Cholesterol 203mg; Calcium 273mg; Fibre 0.8g; Sodium 514mg.

Aromatic tiger prawns

There is no elegant way to eat these aromatic prawns – just hold them by the tails, pull them off the sticks with your fingers and pop them into your mouth.

SERVES 4

16 raw tiger prawns (jumbo shrimp) or scampi
   (extra large shrimp) tails
2.5ml/½ tsp chilli powder
5ml/1 tsp fennel seeds
5 Sichuan or black peppercorns
1 star anise, broken into segments
1 cinnamon stick, broken into pieces
30ml/2 tbsp groundnut or sunflower oil

2 garlic cloves, chopped
2cm/¾in piece fresh root ginger, peeled and
   finely chopped
1 shallot, chopped
30ml/2 tbsp water
30ml/2 tbsp rice vinegar
30ml/2 tbsp soft brown or palm sugar (jaggery)
salt and ground black pepper
lime slices and spring onion (scallion), to garnish

1 If you are using whole prawns, remove the heads. Thread the prawns or scampi tails in pairs on 8 wooden cocktail sticks (toothpicks). Set aside. Heat a frying pan, put in all the chilli powder, fennel seeds, Sichuan or black peppercorns, star anise and cinnamon stick and dry-fry for 1–2 minutes to release the flavours. Leave to cool, then grind coarsely in a grinder or tip into a mortar and crush with a pestle.

2 Heat the groundnut or sunflower oil in a shallow pan, add the garlic, ginger and chopped shallot and then fry gently until very lightly coloured. Add the crushed spices and seasoning and cook the mixture gently for 2 minutes. Pour in the water and simmer, stirring, for 5 minutes.

3 Add the rice vinegar and soft brown or palm sugar, stir until dissolved, then add the prawns or scampi tails. Cook for about 3–5 minutes, until the seafood has turned pink, but is still very juicy. Serve hot, garnished with lime slices and spring onion.

Nutritional information per portion: Energy 142kcal/593kJ; Protein 13.4g; Carbohydrate 9g, of which sugars 8.7g; Fat 6g, of which saturates 0.7g; Cholesterol 146mg; Calcium 67mg; Fibre 0.2g; Sodium 144mg.

Italian prawn skewers

Parsley and lemon are all that is required to create a lovely tiger prawn dish. Grill them, or barbecue them for an informal al fresco summer appetizer.

SERVES 4

900g/2lb raw tiger prawns (jumbo
   shrimp), peeled
60ml/4 tbsp olive oil
45ml/3 tbsp vegetable oil
75g/3oz/1¼ cups very fine
   dry breadcrumbs
1 garlic clove, crushed
15ml/1 tbsp chopped fresh parsley
salt and ground black pepper
lemon wedges, to serve

1 Slit the prawns down their backs and remove the dark vein. Rinse in cold water and dry on kitchen paper.

2 Put the oils in a large bowl and add the prawns, coating them evenly. Add the breadcrumbs, garlic and parsley and season. Toss the prawns thoroughly, to give them an even coating of breadcrumbs. Cover and leave to marinate for 1 hour.

3 Carefully thread the tiger prawns on to four metal or wooden skewers, curling them up as you work, so that the tails are skewered neatly in the middle.

4 Preheat the grill (broiler) to a moderate heat. Place the skewers in the grill (broiling) pan and cook for 2 minutes on each side, until they are golden. Serve with the lemon.

Nutritional information per portion: Energy 415kcal/1734kJ; Protein 42.2g; Carbohydrate 14.9g, of which sugars 0.8g; Fat 21.1g, of which saturates 2.8g; Cholesterol 439mg; Calcium 227mg; Fibre 1.1g; Sodium 574mg.

Prawn cocktail

There is no nicer starter than a good, fresh prawn cocktail – but not with soggy prawns in a thin, vinegary sauce embedded in limp lettuce. This recipe shows how good a prawn cocktail can be.

SERVES 6

60ml/4 tbsp double (heavy) cream, lightly whipped
60ml/4 tbsp mayonnaise, preferably home-made
60ml/4 tbsp tomato ketchup
5–10ml/1–2 tsp Worcestershire sauce
juice of 1 lemon
1/2 cos or romaine lettuce
450g/1lb/4 cups cooked peeled prawns (shrimp)
salt, ground black pepper and paprika
6 large whole cooked unpeeled prawns (shrimp), to garnish (optional)
thinly sliced brown bread and lemon wedges, to serve

1 In a bowl, mix together the whipped cream, mayonnaise and ketchup. Add Worcestershire sauce to taste. Stir in enough lemon juice to make a really tangy sauce.

2 Finely shred the lettuce and fill six individual glasses one-third full. Stir the prawns into the sauce, then check the seasoning. Spoon the prawn mixture over the lettuce.

3 To prepare the garnish, if desired, peel the body shell from the whole cooked prawns and leave the tail "fan" for decoration. Drape one prawn over the edge of each glass. Sprinkle each of the cocktails with ground black pepper and some paprika. Serve immediately, with the thinly sliced brown bread and butter and lemon wedges for squeezing over.

Nutritional information per portion: Energy 194kcal/805kJ; Protein 13.9g; Carbohydrate 4.2g, of which sugars 4g; Fat 13.6g, of which saturates 4.6g; Cholesterol 167mg; Calcium 80mg; Fibre 0.4g; Sodium 384mg.

Hot crab soufflés

These delicious little soufflés must be served as soon as they are ready, so seat your guests at the table before taking the soufflés out of the oven.

SERVES 6

50g/2oz/¼ cup butter
45ml/3 tbsp fine wholemeal
   (whole-wheat) breadcrumbs
4 spring onions (scallions), finely chopped
15ml/1 tbsp Malayan or mild Madras
   curry powder
25g/1oz/2 tbsp plain flour
105ml/7 tbsp coconut milk or milk

150ml/¼ pint/²⁄₃ cup whipping cream
4 egg yolks
225g/8oz white crab meat
mild green Tabasco sauce
6 egg whites
salt and ground black pepper

1 Use some of the butter to grease six ramekin dishes or a 1.75 litre/3 pint/7½ cup soufflé dish. Sprinkle in the fine wholemeal breadcrumbs, roll the dishes or dish around to coat the base and sides completely, then tip out the excess breadcrumbs. Preheat the oven to 200°C/400°F/Gas 6.

2 Melt the remaining butter in a pan, add the spring onions and Malayan or mild Madras curry powder and cook over a low heat for about 1 minute, until softened. Stir in the flour and cook for a further 1 minute.

3 Gradually add the coconut milk or milk and the cream, stirring constantly. Cook until smooth and thick. Off the heat, stir in the egg yolks, then the crab. Season well with salt, black pepper and Tabasco sauce.

4 In a grease-free bowl, beat the egg whites stiffly with a pinch of salt. With a metal spoon stir one-third into the crab mixture then fold in the rest. Spoon into the dishes or dish.

5 Bake until well risen, golden brown and just firm to the touch. Individual soufflés will take 8 minutes; a large soufflé 15–20 minutes. Serve at once.

Nutritional information per portion: Energy 270kcal/1122kJ; Protein 14g; Carbohydrate 11.6g, of which sugars 2.2g; Fat 18.9g, of which saturates 12.1g; Cholesterol 181mg; Calcium 123mg; Fibre 1g; Sodium 426mg.

Crab cakes with tartare sauce

*Sweet crab meat is offset by a piquant sauce. To make the crab go further, add 50g/2oz/1 cup
fresh breadcrumbs and 1 more egg to the crab mixture. Divide into 12 cakes to serve 6.*

SERVES 4

675g/1½ lb fresh crab meat
1 egg, beaten
30ml/2 tbsp mayonnaise
15ml/1 tbsp Worcestershire sauce
15ml/1 tbsp sherry
30ml/2 tbsp fresh parsley,
   finely chopped
15ml/1 tbsp fresh chives or dill,
   finely chopped
salt and ground black pepper
45ml/3 tbsp olive oil
salad leaves and lemon, to garnish

FOR THE SAUCE

1 egg yolk
15ml/1 tbsp white wine vinegar
30ml/2 tbsp Dijon-style mustard
250ml/8fl oz/1 cup vegetable or
   groundnut (peanut) oil
3ml/2 tbsp fresh lemon juice
60ml/4 tbsp spring onions (scallions),
   finely chopped
30ml/2 tbsp chopped drained capers
60ml/4 tbsp dill pickles, finely chopped
60ml/4 tbsp parsley, finely chopped

1 Pick over the crab meat, removing any pieces of shell or
cartilage. In a mixing bowl, combine the beaten egg with
the mayonnaise, Worcestershire sauce, sherry and herbs.
Season with salt and lots of ground black pepper.

2 Gently fold in the crab meat. Divide the mixture into 8
portions and gently form each one into an oval cake. Place
on a baking sheet between layers of baking parchment and
chill for at least 1 hour.

3 Meanwhile, make the sauce. In a medium-size bowl, beat the egg yolk with a wire whisk until
smooth. Add the vinegar, mustard, and salt and pepper to taste, and whisk for about 10 seconds to
blend. Slowly whisk in the oil. Add the lemon juice, spring onions, capers, pickles and parsley, and
mix well. Check the seasoning. Cover and chill.

4 Preheat the grill (broiler). Brush the crab cakes with the olive oil. Place on an oiled baking sheet, in
one layer. Grill (broil) 15cm/6in from the heat until golden brown, for about 5 minutes on each side.
Serve the crab cakes with the tartare sauce, garnished with salad leaves and lemon.

Nutritional information per portion: Energy 701kcal/2899kJ; Protein 33.4g; Carbohydrate 1.4g, of which sugars 1.3g; Fat 62g, of which saturates 8.1g;
Cholesterol 225mg; Calcium 238mg; Fibre 0.4g; Sodium 1029mg.

Mussels and clams with lemon grass

Lemon grass has an incomparable flavour and is excellent used with seafood. If you cannot find clams, use extra mussels instead but buy a few more in case some need to be discarded.

SERVES 6

1.8–2kg/4–4¹/₂ lb mussels
120ml/4fl oz/¹/₂ cup dry white wine
1 bunch spring onions
    (scallions), chopped
2 lemon grass stalks, chopped
6 kaffir lime leaves, chopped
10ml/2 tsp Thai green curry paste
450g/1lb baby clams, washed
200ml/7fl oz/scant 1 cup coconut cream
30ml/2 tbsp chopped fresh coriander
    (cilantro)
salt and ground black pepper
whole garlic chives, to garnish

1 Clean the mussels. Pull off the "beards" and scrub the shells. Discard any that are broken or stay open when tapped.

2 Put the wine, spring onions, lemon grass, lime leaves and curry paste in a pan. Simmer the mixture until the wine almost evaporates.

3 Add the mussels and clams to the pan, cover tightly and steam the shellfish over a high heat for 5–6 minutes, until they open.

4 Using a slotted spoon, transfer the mussels and clams to a warmed serving bowl and keep hot. Discard any shellfish that remain closed. Strain the cooking liquid into a clean pan and then simmer to reduce the amount by half.

5 Stir in the coconut cream and coriander, with salt and pepper to taste. Heat through. Pour over the seafood and serve, garnished with garlic chives.

Nutritional information per portion: Energy 237kcal/993kJ; Protein 22.5g; Carbohydrate 2.8g, of which sugars 1.7g; Fat 13.8g, of which saturates 10.3g; Cholesterol 58mg; Calcium 238mg; Fibre 0.9g; Sodium 606mg.

Scallop-stuffed roast peppers with pesto

Serve these scallop-and-pesto-filled sweet red peppers with Italian bread, such as ciabatta or focaccia, to mop up the tasty juices.

SERVES 4

4 squat red (bell) peppers
2 large garlic cloves, cut into thin slivers
60ml/4 tbsp olive oil
4 shelled scallops
45ml/3 tbsp pesto sauce
salt and ground black pepper
freshly grated Parmesan cheese, to serve
salad leaves and basil sprigs, to garnish

1 Preheat the oven to 180°C/350°F/Gas 4. Cut the peppers in half lengthways, through their stalks. Scrape out and discard the cores and seeds. Wash the pepper shells and pat dry with kitchen paper.

2 Put the peppers, cut-side up, in an oiled roasting pan. Divide the slivers of garlic equally among them and sprinkle with salt and ground black pepper to taste. Then spoon the oil into the peppers and roast for 40 minutes.

3 Using a sharp knife, carefully cut each of the shelled scallops in half horizontally to make two flat discs each with a piece of coral. When cooked, remove the peppers from the oven and place a scallop half in each pepper half. Then top with the pesto sauce.

4 Return the pan to the oven and roast for 10 minutes more. Make sure you don't overcook the scallops otherwise they will become tough and rubbery. Transfer the peppers and scallops to individual serving plates, sprinkle with grated Parmesan and garnish each plate with a few salad leaves and basil sprigs. Serve warm.

Nutritional information per portion: Energy 285kcal/1186kJ; Protein 18.6g; Carbohydrate 16.7g, of which sugars 13.8g; Fat 16.3g, of which saturates 4.3g; Cholesterol 35mg; Calcium 168mg; Fibre 3.8g; Sodium 222mg.

Clams with chilli and yellow bean sauce

This delicious Thai-inspired dish is simple to prepare. It can be made in a matter of minutes so will not keep you away from your guests for very long.

SERVES 4–6

1kg/2¼ lb fresh clams
30ml/2 tbsp vegetable oil
4 garlic cloves, finely chopped
15ml/1 tbsp grated fresh root ginger
4 shallots, finely chopped

30ml/2 tbsp yellow bean sauce
6 red chillies, seeded and chopped
15ml/1 tbsp fish sauce
pinch of sugar
handful of basil leaves, plus extra
    to garnish

1 Wash and scrub the clams. Heat the oil in a wok or large frying pan. Add the garlic and ginger and fry for about 30 seconds, add the shallots and fry for a further minute.

2 Add the clams to the pan. Using a fish slice or spatula, turn them a few times to coat all over with the oil. Add the yellow bean sauce and half the chopped red chillies.

3 Continue to cook, stirring often, for 5–7 minutes, or until all the clams are open. You may need to add a splash of water. Adjust the seasoning with the fish sauce and a little sugar. Finally add the basil leaves and stir to mix.

4 Transfer the clams to a serving platter. Garnish with the remaining chopped red chillies and basil leaves and serve.

Nutritional information per portion: Energy 94kcal/393kJ; Protein 11.6g; Carbohydrate 2.4g, of which sugars 0.6g; Fat 4.3g, of which saturates 0.6g; Cholesterol 45mg; Calcium 75mg; Fibre 0.7g; Sodium 998mg.

Scallop and mussel kebabs

*These delightfully crispy seafood skewers are served with hot toast spread
with a lovely fresh herb butter.*

SERVES 4

65g/2¹/₂oz/5 tbsp butter, at
room temperature
30ml/2 tbsp fresh fennel or parsley,
finely chopped
15ml/1 tbsp lemon juice
32 small scallops, removed from shells

24 large mussels, in the shell
8 bacon rashers
50g/2oz/1 cup fresh breadcrumbs
50ml/2fl oz/¹/₄ cup olive oil
salt and ground black pepper
hot toast, to serve

1 Make the flavoured butter by combining the butter with the chopped
herbs and lemon juice. Add salt and pepper to taste. Mix well and set aside.

2 In a small pan, cook the scallops in their own liquor until they begin to
shrink. (If there is no scallop liquor – retained from the shells after shucking –
use a little fish stock or white wine.) Drain the scallops well and then pat dry
with kitchen paper.

3 Scrub the mussels well and remove their "beards", then rinse under cold
running water. Place in a large pan with about 2.5cm/1in of water in the base.
Cover and steam the mussels over a medium heat until they open. When cool
enough to handle, remove them from their shells, and pat dry using kitchen
paper. Discard any mussels that have not opened during cooking.

4 Take eight 15cm/6in wooden or metal skewers. Thread on each one,
alternately, 4 scallops and 3 mussels. As you are doing this, weave a rasher
of bacon between the scallops and mussels.

5 Preheat the grill (broiler). Spread the breadcrumbs on a plate. Brush the
seafood with olive oil and roll in the crumbs to coat all over.

6 Place the skewers on the grill (broiling) rack. Cook until crisp and lightly
browned, 4–5 minutes on each side. Serve immediately with hot toast and
the flavoured butter.

Nutritional information per portion. Energy 506kcal/2108kJ; Protein 37.4g; Carbohydrate 14.4g, of which sugars 0.6g;
Fat 33.6g, of which saturates 13.7g; Cholesterol 130mg; Calcium 75mg; Fibre 0.6g; Sodium 1414mg.

Salmon and scallop brochettes

With their delicate pastel colours and really superb flavour, these skewers make the perfect opener for a sophisticated dinner party.

SERVES 4

225g/8oz salmon fillet, skinned
8 shucked queen scallops, with their
   corals if possible
8 baby onions, peeled and blanched
1/2 yellow (bell) pepper, cut into
   8 squares
8 lemon grass stalks
25g/1oz/2 tbsp butter
juice of 1/2 lemon
salt, ground white pepper and paprika

FOR THE SAUCE
30ml/2 tbsp dry vermouth
50g/2oz/1/4 cup butter
5ml/1 tsp chopped fresh tarragon

1 Preheat the grill (broiler) to medium-high. Cut the salmon into 12 2cm/3/4 in cubes. Thread the salmon, scallops, corals, onions and pepper squares on to the lemon grass stalks and place the brochettes in a grill (broiling) pan.

2 Melt the butter, add the lemon juice and a pinch of paprika and then brush over the brochettes. Grill (broil) the skewers for 2–3 minutes on each side, turning and basting the brochettes twice, until the fish and scallops are just cooked. Keep hot while you make the sauce.

3 Pour the dry vermouth and the leftover cooking juices from the brochettes into a small pan and boil fiercely to reduce by half. Add the butter and melt, then add the tarragon and salt and pepper. Serve the sauce with the brochettes.

Nutritional information per portion: Energy 321kcal/1336kJ; Protein 23.5g; Carbohydrate 4.8g, of which sugars 2.7g; Fat 22.4g, of which saturates 11.1g; Cholesterol 92mg; Calcium 36mg; Fibre 0.6g; Sodium 231mg.

Marinated asparagus and langoustine

For a really extravagant treat, you could make this attractive salad with medallions of lobster.
For a cheaper version, use large prawns, allowing six per serving.

SERVES 4

16 langoustines
16 fresh asparagus spears, trimmed
2 carrots
30ml/2 tbsp olive oil
1 garlic clove, peeled
salt and ground black pepper
4 fresh tarragon sprigs and some
chopped, to garnish

FOR THE DRESSING

30ml/2 tbsp tarragon vinegar
120ml/4fl oz/1/2 cup olive oil

1 Peel the langoustines and keep the discarded parts for stock.

2 Steam the asparagus over boiling salted water until just tender. Refresh under cold water, drain and place in a shallow dish.

3 Peel the carrots and cut into fine julienne shreds. Cook in a pan of lightly salted boiling water for about 3 minutes, until tender but still crunchy. Drain, refresh under cold water, drain again. Add the carrots to the asparagus.

4 For the dressing, whisk the vinegar with the oil. Season to taste. Pour over the asparagus and carrots and leave to marinate.

5 Heat the oil with the garlic in a frying pan until very hot. Add the langoustines and sauté until just heated through. Discard the garlic.

6 Divide the asparagus and carrots among four plates. Drizzle with the rest of the dressing and top each with four langoustine tails. Add the chopped tarragon and sprigs. Serve.

Nutritional information per portion. Energy 328kcal/1357kJ; Protein 20.7g; Carbohydrate 4g, of which sugars 3.8g; Fat 25.5g, of which saturates 3.7g; Cholesterol 195mg; Calcium 112mg; Fibre 2.3g; Sodium 197mg.

Garlic prawns in filo tartlets

Tartlets made with crisp golden layers of filo pastry and filled with spicy garlic and chilli prawns make a tempting starter, suitable for all occasions.

SERVES 4

FOR THE TARTLETS
50g/2oz/4 tbsp butter, melted
2–3 large sheets filo pastry

FOR THE FILLING
115g/4oz/½ cup butter

2–3 garlic cloves, crushed
1 red chilli, seeded and chopped
350g/12oz/3 cups cooked peeled
    prawns (shrimp)
30ml/2 tbsp chopped fresh parsley or
    chopped fresh chives
    salt and ground black pepper

1 Preheat the oven to 200°C/400°F/Gas 6. Brush four individual 7.5cm/3in flan tins (pans) with the melted butter.

2 Cut the filo pastry into twelve 10cm/4in squares and brush with the melted butter. Place three squares of pastry inside each tin, overlapping them at slight angles and carefully frilling the edges and points while forming a good hollow in each centre.

3 Bake in the oven for 10–15 minutes, until crisp and golden. Leave to cool slightly then remove the pastry cases from the tins.

4 Meanwhile, make the filling. Melt the butter in a frying pan, then add the garlic, chilli and prawns and fry quickly for 1–2 minutes to warm through. Stir in the parsley or chives and season with salt and plenty of pepper. Spoon the prawn filling into the tartlets and serve at once.

Nutritional information per portion: Energy 440kcal/1825kJ; Protein 17.6g; Carbohydrate 15g, of which sugars 0.7g; Fat 34.8g, of which saturates 21.6g; Cholesterol 259mg; Calcium 118mg; Fibre 1g; Sodium 419mg.

Poultry and meat

Tasty and spicy bites of meat served

as parcels, kebabs, meatballs or pies

are popular in many different cultures

around the world, including North Africa,

Indonesia, Japan and India. Meat can also

be included in more substantial appetizers

such as a delicious creamy Italian risotto.

Golden Parmesan chicken

Served cold with the garlicky mayonnaise, these morsels of Parmesan-coated chicken make a great appetizer, especially if served informally as finger food.

SERVES 4

4 chicken breast fillets, skinned
75g/3oz/1¹⁄₂ cups fresh
    white breadcrumbs
40g/1¹⁄₂ oz Parmesan cheese,
    finely grated
30ml/2 tbsp chopped fresh parsley
2 eggs, beaten
120ml/4fl oz/¹⁄₂ cup mayonnaise
120ml/4fl oz/¹⁄₂ cup fromage frais (low-
    fat cream cheese)
1–2 garlic cloves, crushed
50g/2oz/4 tbsp butter, melted
salt and ground black pepper

1 Cut each fillet into four or five chunks. Mix together the breadcrumbs, Parmesan, parsley and seasoning in a shallow dish. Dip the chicken pieces in the egg, then into the breadcrumb mixture. Place in a single layer on a baking sheet; chill for 30 minutes.

2 To make the garlic mayonnaise, mix together the mayonnaise, fromage frais and garlic, and season to taste. Spoon into a small serving bowl. Chill.

3 Preheat the oven to 180°C/350°F/Gas 4. Drizzle the melted butter over the chicken pieces and cook them for about 20 minutes, until crisp and golden. Serve the chicken accompanied by the garlic mayonnaise for dipping.

Nutritional information per portion: Energy 591kcal/2460kJ; Protein 35.7g; Carbohydrate 16.7g, of which sugars 2.4g; Fat 43g, of which saturates 14.7g; Cholesterol 227mg; Calcium 216mg; Fibre 0.8g; Sodium 571mg.

Chicken with lemon and garlic

Extremely easy to cook and delicious to eat, this succulent tapas dish makes a great last-minute starter and tastes even better served with some home-made aioli.

SERVES 4

225g/8oz skinless chicken breast fillets
30ml/2 tbsp olive oil
1 shallot, finely chopped
4 garlic cloves, finely chopped
5ml/1 tsp paprika
juice of 1 lemon
30ml/2 tbsp chopped fresh parsley
salt and ground black pepper
flat leaf parsley, to garnish
lemon wedges, to serve

1 Sandwich the chicken breast fillets between two sheets of clear film (plastic wrap) or baking parchment. Bat out with a rolling pin or meat mallet until the fillets are about 5mm/¼in thick.

2 Cut the chicken into strips about 1cm/½ in wide. Heat the oil in a large frying pan. Stir-fry the chicken strips with the shallot, garlic and paprika over a high heat for about 3 minutes until lightly browned and cooked through. Add the lemon juice and parsley with salt and pepper to taste. Serve with lemon wedges, garnished with flat leaf parsley.

Nutritional information per portion: Energy 119kcal/496kJ; Protein 14.1g; Carbohydrate 1.5g, of which sugars 1.1g; Fat 6.3g, of which saturates 1g; Cholesterol 39mg; Calcium 32mg; Fibre 0.8g; Sodium 38mg.

Tandoori chicken sticks

This aromatic chicken dish is traditionally baked in a special clay oven called a tandoor. Here, the chicken is marinated and then grilled, with truly excellent results.

MAKES ABOUT 25

450g/1lb skinless chicken breast fillets

FOR THE CORIANDER YOGURT
250ml/8fl oz/1 cup natural (plain) yogurt
30ml/2 tbsp whipping cream
1/2 cucumber, peeled, seeded and
    finely chopped
15–30ml/1–2 tbsp fresh chopped mint
    or coriander (cilantro)
salt and ground black pepper

FOR THE MARINADE
175ml/6fl oz/3/4 cup natural
    (plain) yogurt
5ml/1 tsp garam masala or curry powder
1.5ml/1/4 tsp ground cumin
1.5ml/1/4 tsp ground coriander
1.5ml/1/4 tsp cayenne pepper (or
    to taste)
5ml/1 tsp tomato purée (paste)
1–2 garlic cloves, finely chopped
2.5cm/1in piece fresh root ginger, peeled
    and finely chopped
grated rind and juice of 1/2 lemon
15–30ml/1–2 tbsp chopped fresh mint

1 Prepare the coriander yogurt. Combine all the ingredients in a bowl and season with salt and ground black pepper. Cover with clear film (plastic wrap) and chill until you are ready to serve.

2 Prepare the marinade. Place all the ingredients in the bowl of a food processor, and process thoroughly until the mixture is smooth. Pour into a shallow dish.

3 Freeze the chicken breasts for 5 minutes to firm, then slice in half horizontally. Cut the slices into 2cm/3/4in strips and add to the marinade. Toss to coat well. Cover and chill in the fridge for 6–8 hours or overnight.

4 Preheat the grill (broiler) and line a baking sheet with foil. Using a slotted spoon, remove the chicken from the marinade and arrange the pieces in a single layer on the baking sheet. Scrunch up the chicken slightly so it makes wavy shapes. Grill for 4–5 minutes until brown and just cooked, turning once. When cool enough to handle, thread 1–2 pieces on to cocktail sticks (toothpicks) or short skewers and serve with the coriander yogurt dip.

Nutritional information per portion: Energy 32kcal/134kJ; Protein 5g; Carbohydrate 1.1g, of which sugars 0.8g; Fat 0.9g, of which saturates 0.4g; Cholesterol 14mg; Calcium 29mg; Fibre 0.2g; Sodium 23mg.

Barbecue-glazed chicken skewers

Known as yakitori *in Japan, these aromatic chicken and spring onion skewers are popular throughout the country and are often served as an appetizer with drinks.*

MAKES 12 SKEWERS AND 8 WING PIECES

8 chicken wings
4 chicken thighs, skinned
4 spring onions (scallions), blanched and
   cut into short lengths

FOR THE BASTING SAUCE
60ml/4 tbsp sake
75ml/5 tbsp/¹⁄₃ cup dark soy sauce
30ml/2 tbsp tamari sauce
15ml/1 tbsp mirin, or sweet sherry
15ml/1 tbsp sugar

1 Remove the wing tip of the chicken at the first joint. Chop through the second joint, revealing the two narrow bones. Take hold of the bones with a clean cloth and pull, turning the meat around the bones inside out. Remove the smaller bone and discard. Set the wings aside. Bone the chicken thighs and cut the meat into large dice. Thread the spring onions and thigh meat on to 12 skewers.

2 Measure the basting sauce ingredients into a stainless-steel or enamel pan and simmer until reduced by two-thirds. Cool.

3 Heat the grill (broiler) to a moderately high temperature. Grill (broil) the skewers without applying any oil. When juices begin to emerge from the chicken, baste liberally with the sauce. Allow a further 3 minutes for the chicken on skewers and not more than 5 minutes for the wings.

Nutritional information per portion: Energy 98kcal/415kJ; Protein 20.3g; Carbohydrate 1.9g, of which sugars 1.9g; Fat 0.9g, of which saturates 0.3g; Cholesterol 58mg; Calcium 7mg; Fibre 0.1g; Sodium 495mg.

Chicken parcels

These home-made chicken parcels look splendid piled high and golden brown. Flavoured with parsley and nutmeg, they will be an instant success with your guests.

MAKES 35

225g/8oz/2 cups strong white bread
  flour, plus extra for dusting
2.5ml/¹/₂ tsp salt
2.5ml/¹/₂ tsp caster (superfine) sugar
5ml/1 tsp easy-blend dried
  (rapid-rise) yeast
25g/1oz/2 tbsp butter, softened
1 egg, beaten, plus a little extra
90ml/6 tbsp warm milk
lemon wedges, to serve

FOR THE FILLING

1 small onion, finely chopped
175g/6oz/1¹/₂ cups minced chicken
15ml/1 tbsp sunflower oil
75ml/5 tbsp chicken stock
30ml/2 tbsp chopped fresh parsley
pinch of grated nutmeg
salt and ground black pepper

1 Sift the flour, salt and sugar into a large bowl. Stir in the dried yeast, then make a well in the centre of the flour. Add the butter, egg and milk and mix to a soft dough. Turn on to a lightly floured surface and knead for 10 minutes, until the dough is smooth and elastic. Put the dough in a clean bowl, cover with clear film (plastic wrap) and then leave in a warm place to rise for 1 hour, or until the dough has doubled in size.

2 Meanwhile, fry the onion and chicken in the oil for about 10 minutes. Add the stock and simmer for 5 minutes. Stir in the parsley, grated nutmeg and salt and ground black pepper. Then leave to cool.

3 Preheat the oven to 220°C/425°F/Gas 7. Knead the dough, then roll it out until it is 3mm/¹/₈in thick. Stamp out rounds with a 7.5cm/3in cutter. Brush the edges with beaten egg. Put a little filling in the middle, then press the edges together. Leave to rise on oiled baking sheets, covered with oiled clear film (plastic wrap), for 15 minutes. Brush with more egg. Bake for 5 minutes, then for 10 minutes at 190°C/375°F/Gas 5, until well risen. Serve with lemon wedges.

Nutritional information per portion: Energy 554kcal/2310kJ; Protein 42.5g; Carbohydrate 14.8g, of which sugars 0.5g; Fat 36.6g, of which saturates 22g; Cholesterol 240mg; Calcium 138mg; Fibre 0.6g; Sodium 417mg.

Chicken bitki

This is a popular dish in its native country, Poland, and makes an attractive starter when offset by deep red beetroot and vibrant green salad leaves.

MAKES 12

15g/¹⁄₂oz/1 tbsp butter, melted
115g/4oz flat mushrooms, finely chopped
50g/2oz/1 cup fresh white breadcrumbs
350g/12oz chicken breast fillets, minced
(ground) or finely chopped
2 eggs, separated
1.5ml/¹⁄₄ tsp grated nutmeg
30ml/2 tbsp plain (all-purpose) flour
45ml/3 tbsp oil
salt and ground black pepper
salad leaves and grated pickled beetroot
(beet), to serve

1 Melt the butter in a pan and fry the mushrooms for about 5 minutes until soft and the juices have evaporated. Allow to cool.

2 Mix the mushrooms and the breadcrumbs, the chicken, egg yolks, nutmeg, salt and pepper together.

3 Whisk the egg whites until they are stiff. Stir half of the egg whites into the chicken mixture to slacken it, then fold in the remainder. Shape into 12 even meatballs, about 7.5cm/3in long and about 2.5cm/1in wide. Roll in the flour to coat evenly.

4 Heat the oil in a frying pan and fry the bitki for about 10 minutes, turning until evenly golden brown and cooked through. Serve hot with some salad leaves and the grated pickled beetroot.

Nutritional information per portion: Energy 102kcal/426kJ; Protein 8.9g; Carbohydrate 5.2g, of which sugars 0.2g; Fat 5.2g, of which saturates 1.3g; Cholesterol 55mg; Calcium 16mg; Fibre 0.3g; Sodium 69mg.

Risotto alla Milanese

This classic risotto is often served with the hearty beef stew, osso buco, but it also makes a delicious first course in its own right.

SERVES 5–6

about 1.2 litres/2 pints/5 cups beef or
    chicken stock
good pinch of saffron threads
75g/3oz/6 tbsp butter
1 onion, finely chopped
275g/10oz/1½ cups risotto rice
75g/3oz/1 cup freshly grated
    Parmesan cheese
salt and ground black pepper

1 Bring the stock to the boil, then reduce to a low simmer. Ladle a little stock into a small bowl. Add the saffron and leave to infuse.

2 Melt 50g/2oz/4 tbsp of the butter in a large pan. Add the onion and cook gently for about 3 minutes until softened but not browned.

3 Add the rice. Stir until the grains start to swell and burst, then add a few ladlefuls of the stock, with the saffron liquid and seasoning. Stir over a low heat until the stock has

been absorbed. Add the remaining stock, a few ladlefuls at a time, allowing the rice to absorb all the liquid before adding more, and stirring constantly. After about 20–25 minutes, the rice should be just tender and creamy.

4 Stir in about two-thirds of the grated Parmesan and the remaining butter. Heat through until the butter has melted. Transfer the risotto to a warmed serving bowl or platter and serve hot, with the remaining grated Parmesan served separately.

Nutritional information per portion: Energy 397kcal/1650kJ; Protein 10.6g; Carbohydrate 46.8g, of which sugars 0.0g; Fat 18.3g, of which saturates 11.3g; Cholesterol 49mg; Calcium 204mg; Fibre 0.2g; Sodium 265mg.

Lamb tikka

Creamy yogurt and ground nuts go wonderfully with the spices in these little Indian meatballs.
If you intend to use wooden skewers, soak them in cold water for 30 minutes before cooking.

MAKES ABOUT 20

450g/1lb lamb fillet
2 spring onions (scallions), chopped

FOR THE MARINADE
350ml/12 fl oz/1¹/₂ cups natural
    (plain) yogurt
15ml/1 tbsp ground almonds, cashew
    nuts or peanuts

15ml/1 tbsp vegetable oil
2–3 garlic cloves, finely chopped
juice of 1 lemon
5ml/1 tsp garam masala or curry powder
2.5ml/¹/₂ tsp ground cardamom
1.5ml/¹/₄ tsp cayenne pepper
15–30ml/1–2 tbsp chopped fresh mint

1 To prepare the marinade, stir together the marinade ingredients. In a separate small bowl, reserve about 120ml/4fl oz/¹/₂ cup of the mixture to use as a dipping sauce for the meatballs.

2 Cut the lamb into small pieces and put in the bowl of a food processor with the spring onions. Process until the meat is finely chopped. Add 30–45ml/2–3 tbsp of the marinade and process again. Test to see if the mixture holds together by pinching a little between your fingertips. Add a little more marinade if necessary, but do not make the mixture too wet and soft.

3 With moistened palms, form the meat mixture into slightly oval-shaped balls, measuring about 4cm/1¹/₂in long, and then arrange the meatballs in a shallow ovenproof dish.

4 Spoon over the remaining marinade. Chill the meatballs in the fridge for 8–10 hours or overnight.

5 Soak 20 wooden skewers for 30 minutes. Preheat the grill (broiler) and line a baking sheet with foil. Thread each meatball on to a skewer and arrange on the baking sheet.

6 Grill (broil) for 4–5 minutes, turning them occasionally, until crisp and golden on all sides. Serve with the marinade as a dipping sauce.

Nutritional information per portion: Energy 44kcal/182kJ; Protein 4.7g; Carbohydrate 0.4g, of which sugars 0.3g; Fat 2.6g, of which saturates 1.2g; Cholesterol 17mg; Calcium 12mg; Fibre 0.1g; Sodium 25mg.

Deep-fried lamb patties

These patties are a tasty North African speciality – called kibbeh – of minced meat and bulgur wheat. They are sometimes stuffed with additional meat and deep fried.

SERVES 6

450g/1lb lean lamb or lean minced
    (ground) lamb or beef
salt and ground black pepper
oil, for deep-frying
avocado slices and coriander (cilantro)
    sprigs, to serve

FOR THE PATTIES
225g/8oz/1¹⁄₃ cups bulgur wheat
1 red chilli, seeded and roughly chopped
1 onion, roughly chopped

FOR THE STUFFING
1 onion, finely chopped
50g/2oz/²⁄₃ cup pine nuts
30ml/2 tbsp olive oil
7.5ml/1¹⁄₂ tsp ground allspice
60ml/4 tbsp chopped fresh
    coriander (cilantro)

1 Cut up the lamb and mince (grind) the pieces in a blender or food processor. Divide the minced meat into two equal portions.

2 For the patties, soak the bulgur wheat for 15 minutes in cold water. Drain then process in a blender or a food processor with the chilli, onion, half the meat and salt and pepper.

3 For the stuffing, fry the onion and pine nuts in the oil for 5 minutes. Add the allspice and remaining minced (ground) meat and fry gently, breaking up the meat with a wooden spoon, until browned. Stir in the coriander and seasoning. Shape the patty mixture into a cake. Cut into 12 wedges. Flatten one piece and spoon some stuffing into the centre. Bring the edges of the patty up over the stuffing, ensuring that the filling is completely encased.

4 Heat oil to a depth of 5cm/2in in a large pan until a few patty crumbs sizzle on the surface.

5 Lower half of the filled patties into the oil and fry for about 5 minutes until golden. Drain on kitchen paper and keep hot while cooking the remainder. Serve with avocado slices and coriander sprigs.

Nutritional information per portion: Energy 451kcal/1873kJ; Protein 19.2g; Carbohydrate 33.8g, of which sugars 1.6g; Fat 27.5g, of which saturates 5.9g; Cholesterol 57mg; Calcium 17mg; Fibre 1.2g; Sodium 66mg.

Spicy koftas

These koftas are cooked in batches and kept hot. Left-over koftas can be coarsely chopped and packed into pitta bread with chutney or relish for a delicious snack.

MAKES 20–25

450g/1lb lean minced (ground) beef
   or lamb
30ml/2 tbsp finely ground ginger
30ml/2 tbsp finely chopped garlic
4 green chillies, finely chopped
1 small onion, finely chopped
1 egg
2.5ml/¹/2 tsp turmeric
5ml/1 tsp garam masala
50g/2oz coriander (cilantro)
leaves, chopped
4–6 mint leaves, chopped, or
   2.5ml/¹/2 tsp mint sauce
175g/6oz raw potato
salt, to taste
vegetable oil, for deep frying

1 Place the beef or lamb in a large bowl along with the ginger, garlic, chillies, onion, egg, spices and herbs. Grate the potato into the bowl, and season with salt. Knead together to blend well and form a soft dough.

2 Using your fingers, shape the kofta mixture into portions the size of golf balls. You should be able to make 20 to 25 koftas. Leave the balls to rest at room temperature for about 25 minutes.

3 In a wok or frying pan, heat the oil to medium-hot and fry the koftas in small batches until they are golden brown in colour. Drain well and serve hot.

Nutritional information per portion: Energy 96kcal/404kJ; Protein 5.2g; Carbohydrate 11.8g, of which sugars 1.2g; Fat 3.4g, of which saturates 1.4g; Cholesterol 18mg; Calcium 16mg; Fibre 1g; Sodium 28mg.

Pork satay

Originating in Indonesia, satay are skewers of meat marinated with spices and cooked quickly over charcoal. It's street food at its best, but it makes a great-tasting starter too.

MAKES ABOUT 20

450g/1lb lean pork
5ml/1 tsp grated fresh root ginger
1 lemon grass stalk, finely chopped
3 garlic cloves, finely chopped
15ml/1 tbsp medium curry paste
5ml/1 tsp ground cumin
5ml/1 tsp ground turmeric
60ml/4 tbsp coconut cream
30ml/2 tbsp fish sauce
5ml/1 tsp sugar
oil, for brushing
fresh herbs, to garnish

FOR THE SATAY SAUCE

250ml/8fl oz/1 cup coconut milk
30ml/2 tbsp red curry paste
75g/3oz crunchy peanut butter
120ml/4fl oz/1/2 cup chicken stock
45ml/3 tbsp soft light brown sugar
30ml/2 tbsp tamarind juice
15ml/1 tbsp fish sauce
2.5ml/1/2 tsp salt

1 Cut the pork thinly into 5cm/2in strips. Mix together the fresh root ginger, lemon grass, garlic, curry paste, cumin, turmeric, coconut cream, fish sauce and sugar. Pour over the pork and leave to marinate for about 2 hours.

2 Meanwhile, make the sauce. Heat the coconut milk over a medium heat, then add the red curry paste, peanut butter, chicken stock and sugar.

3 Cook and stir until the sauce is smooth, about 5–6 minutes. Add the tamarind juice, fish sauce and salt to taste.

4 Thread the meat on to skewers. Brush with oil and cook over charcoal or under a preheated grill (broiler) for 3–4 minutes on each side, turning occasionally, until cooked and golden brown.

5 Serve with the satay sauce garnished with fresh herbs.

Nutritional information per portion: Energy 83kcal/346kJ; Protein 6g; Carbohydrate 3.6g, of which sugars 3.1g; Fat 5g, of which saturates 2.6g; Cholesterol 14mg; Calcium 13mg; Fibre 0.4g; Sodium 243mg.

Savoury pork pies

These little pies come from Spain and are fun to eat. They look really appetizing served warm in a basket lined with a napkin.

MAKES 12 PASTRIES

350g/12oz shortcrust pastry, thawed
    if frozen

FOR THE FILLING
15ml/1 tbsp vegetable oil
1 onion, chopped
1 clove garlic, crushed
5ml/1 tsp thyme

115g/4oz/1 cup minced (ground) pork
5ml/1 tsp paprika
1 hard-boiled egg, chopped
1 gherkin, chopped
30ml/2 tbsp chopped fresh parsley
vegetable oil, for deep-frying
salt and ground black pepper

1 To make the filling, heat the vegetable oil in a saucepan or wok and soften the onion, garlic and thyme without browning, for about 3–4 minutes. Add the pork and paprika then brown evenly for 6–8 minutes. Season well, turn out into a bowl and cool. When the mixture is cool, add the hard-boiled egg, gherkin and parsley.

2 Turn the pastry out on to a floured work surface and roll out to a 38cm/15in square. Cut out 12 circles 13cm/5in in diameter. Place 15ml/1 tbsp of the filling on each circle, moisten the edges with a little water, fold over and seal.

3 Heat the vegetable oil in a deep-fryer fitted with a basket, to 196°C/385°F. Place three pies at a time in the basket and deep-fry until golden brown. Frying should take at least 1 minute or the inside filling will not be heated through. Serve warm.

Nutritional information per portion: Energy 209kcal/868kJ; Protein 4.2g; Carbohydrate 14.2g, of which sugars 0.7g; Fat 15.4g, of which saturates 3.8g; Cholesterol 26mg; Calcium 38mg; Fibre 0.9g; Sodium 131mg.

Mini sausage rolls

These miniature versions of old-fashioned sausage rolls are always popular – the Parmesan cheese gives them an extra special flavour.

MAKES ABOUT 48

15g/¹/₂ oz/1 tbsp butter

1 onion, finely chopped

350g/12oz good quality sausage meat
   (bulk sausage)

15ml/1 tbsp dried mixed herbs such as
   oregano, thyme, sage, tarragon or dill

25g/1oz finely chopped pistachio
   nuts (optional)

350g/12oz puff pastry, thawed if frozen

60–90ml/4–6 tbsp freshly grated
   Parmesan cheese

salt and ground black pepper

1 egg, lightly beaten, for glazing

poppy seeds, sesame seeds, fennel seeds
   and aniseeds, for sprinkling

mustard, to serve

1 In a small frying pan, over a medium heat, melt the butter. Add the onion and cook for about 5 minutes, until softened. Remove from the heat and cool. Put the onion, sausagemeat, herbs, salt and pepper and nuts (if using) in a mixing bowl and stir together until completely blended.

2 Divide the mixture into 4 equal portions and roll into thin sausages measuring about 25cm/10in long. Set aside. On a lightly floured surface, roll out the pastry to about 3mm/¹/₈in thick. Cut the pastry into 4 strips 25 x 7.5cm/10 x 3in long. Place a long sausage on each pastry strip and sprinkle each with a little Parmesan cheese.

3 Brush one long edge of each of the pastry strips with the egg glaze and roll up to enclose each sausage. Set them seam-side down and press gently to seal. Brush each with the egg glaze and sprinkle with one type of seed. Repeat with remaining pastry strips, using different seeds.

4 Preheat the oven to 220°C/425°F/Gas 7. Lightly grease a large baking sheet. Cut each of the pastry logs into 2.5cm/1in lengths and arrange on the baking sheet. Bake for about 15 minutes until the pastry is crisp and brown. Serve warm, with a pot of mustard to hand.

Nutritional information per portion: Energy 59kcal/245kJ; Protein 1.8g; Carbohydrate 3.7g, of which sugars 0.3g; Fat 4.3g, of which saturates 1.2g; Cholesterol 9mg; Calcium 24mg; Fibre 0.1g; Sodium 99mg.

Quail's eggs in aspic with prosciutto

These eggs, set attractively in aspic, are so easy to make, and are great for summer eating. Serve them with salad leaves and some home-made mayonnaise on the side.

MAKES 12

22g/³⁄₄oz packet aspic powder
45ml/3 tbsp dry sherry
12 quail's eggs
12 fresh coriander (cilantro) or flat
    leaf parsley leaves
6 slices of prosciutto
salad leaves, to serve

1 Make up the aspic following the instructions but replacing 45ml/3 tbsp water with sherry. Leave in the fridge until it begins to thicken.

2 Put the quail's eggs in a pan of cold water and bring to the boil. Boil for 1¹⁄₂ minutes, pour off the hot water and add cold water. When cold, the yolks should be a little soft and the whites firm.

3 Rinse 12 dariole moulds and place them on a tray. Place a herb leaf in the base of each mould, then add an egg. As the aspic thickens add enough to almost cover each egg. Cut the prosciutto into 12 pieces. Fold to fit into the moulds. Put a slice of ham on each egg and pour in the rest of the aspic to fill the mould. Leave for 4 hours until set.

4 To serve, run a knife around the top rim of the aspic. Dip the moulds into warm water and tap gently until loosened. Invert on to small plates and serve with salad leaves.

Nutritional information per portion: Energy 31kcal/129kJ; Protein 3.9g; Carbohydrate 0.2g, of which sugars 0.2g; Fat 1.2g, of which saturates 0.3g; Cholesterol 36mg; Calcium 8mg; Fibre 0.1g; Sodium 97mg.

Eggs benedict

There is still debate over who created this recipe but the most likely story credits a Mr and Mrs LeGrand Benedict, who were regulars at New York's Delmonico's restaurant.

SERVES 4

5ml/1 tsp vinegar
4 eggs
2 English muffins or 4 rounds of bread
butter, for spreading
4 thick slices cooked ham, trimmed to fit
    the muffins
fresh chives, to garnish

FOR THE SAUCE

3 egg yolks
30ml/2 tbsp fresh lemon juice
1.5ml/¼ tsp salt
115g/4oz/½ cup butter
30ml/2 tbsp single (light) cream
ground black pepper

1 To make the sauce, blend the egg yolks, lemon juice and salt in a food processor or blender for 15 seconds.

2 Melt the butter in a saucepan until it bubbles. With the motor running, pour the butter into the food processor. Scrape the sauce into the top of a double boiler, over simmering water. Stir until thickened. (If it curdles, whisk in 15ml/1 tbsp boiling water.) Add the cream and pepper. Keep warm.

3 Bring a shallow pan of water to the boil. Stir in the vinegar. Break each egg into a cup, then slide it into the water. Gently turn the white around the yolk with a slotted spoon. Cook the eggs about 3–4 minutes. Remove from the pan and drain on kitchen paper. Gently trim any ragged edges with scissors.

4 While the eggs are poaching, split and toast the muffins or bread slices. Butter while still warm.

5 Place a piece of ham on each muffin half or slice of toast. Add an egg and spoon over the warm sauce. Garnish with chives and serve.

Nutritional information per portion: Energy 553kcal/2304kJ; Protein 19.8g; Carbohydrate 31.6g, of which sugars 2.2g; Fat 39.7g, of which saturates 18.9g; Cholesterol 427mg; Calcium 148mg; Fibre 1.3g; Sodium 635mg.

Salads

Making a salad is usually very simple and quick, as there is little cooking involved and the vibrant colours of the fresh ingredients add enormously to the pleasure of eating them. Try a simple classic such as Melon and Prosciutto Salad or a more substantial option such as Smoked Trout Pasta Salad.

Goat's cheese salad

Goat's cheese has a strong, tangy flavour, so choose robust salad leaves to accompany it. This dish looks lovely if you use a mixture of different colours and textures for the salad.

SERVES 4

30ml/2 tbsp olive oil

4 slices of French bread, 1cm/¹/₂in thick

8 cups mixed salad leaves, such as frisée
    lettuce, radicchio and red oak leaf, torn
    in small pieces

4 firm goat's cheese rounds, about
    50g/2oz each, rind removed

1 yellow or red (bell) pepper, seeded and
    finely diced

1 small red onion, thinly sliced

45ml/3 tbsp chopped fresh parsley

30ml/2 tbsp chopped fresh chives

FOR THE DRESSING

30ml/2 tbsp white wine vinegar

1.5ml/¹/₄ tsp salt

5ml/1 tsp wholegrain mustard

75ml/5 tbsp olive oil

ground black pepper

1 For the dressing, mix the vinegar and salt with a fork until dissolved. Stir in the mustard. Gradually stir in the olive oil until blended. Season with pepper and set aside until needed.

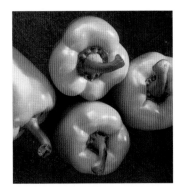

2 Preheat the grill (broiler). Heat the oil in a frying pan. When hot, add the bread slices and fry until golden, about 1 minute. Turn and cook on the other side, about 30 seconds more. Drain on kitchen paper and set aside.

3 Place the salad leaves in a bowl. Add 45ml/3 tbsp of the dressing and toss to coat well. Divide the dressed leaves among four salad plates.

4 Place the goat's cheeses, cut sides up, on a baking sheet and place on the grill (broiler). Grill (broil) until bubbling and golden, about 1–2 minutes.

5 Set a goat's cheese on each slice of bread and place in the centre of each plate. Scatter the diced pepper, red onion, parsley and chives over the salad. Drizzle with the remaining dressing and serve.

Nutritional information per portion: Energy 471kcal/1960kJ; Protein 15.8g; Carbohydrate 27.8g, of which sugars 6.3g; Fat 33.7g, of which saturates 12g; Cholesterol 47mg; Calcium 173mg; Fibre 3.3g; Sodium 555mg.

Panzanella salad

If sliced, juicy tomatoes layered with day-old bread sounds strange for a salad, don't be deceived – it's quite delicious. A popular Italian salad, this dish is ideal for serving as an appetizer.

SERVES 4–6

4 thick slices day-old bread, either
    white, brown or rye
1 small red onion, thinly sliced
450g/1lb ripe tomatoes, thinly sliced
115g/4oz mozzarella cheese, thinly sliced
5ml/1 tbsp fresh basil, shredded, or
    fresh marjoram
120ml/4fl oz/¹/₂ cup extra virgin olive oil
45ml/3 tbsp balsamic vinegar
juice of 1 small lemon
salt and ground black pepper
stoned (pitted) and sliced black olives
    or salted capers, to garnish

1 Dip the bread briefly in cold water, then carefully squeeze out the excess water. Arrange the bread in the base of a shallow salad bowl.

2 Soak the onion slices in cold water for about 10 minutes while you prepare the other ingredients. Drain and reserve.

3 Layer the tomatoes, cheese, onion, basil or marjoram, seasoning well in between each layer. Sprinkle with oil, vinegar and lemon juice.

4 Top with the olives or capers, cover with clear film (plastic wrap) and chill in the fridge for at least 2 hours or overnight, if possible.

Nutritional information per portion: Energy 237kcal/987kJ; Protein 6.3g; Carbohydrate 15.4g, of which sugars 3.5g; Fat 17.1g, of which saturates 4.5g; Cholesterol 11mg; Calcium 105mg; Fibre 1.3g; Sodium 213mg.

Caesar salad

This is a well-known and much-enjoyed salad, even though its origins are a mystery. Be sure to use cos lettuce and add the very soft eggs at the last minute.

SERVES 6

175ml/6fl oz/³⁄₄ cup salad oil, preferably
    olive oil
115g/4oz French or Italian bread, cut in
    2.5cm/1in cubes
1 large garlic clove, crushed with the flat
    side of a knife
1 cos or romaine lettuce
2 eggs, boiled for 1 minute
120ml/4fl oz/¹⁄₂ cup lemon juice
50g/2oz/²⁄₃ cup freshly grated
    Parmesan cheese
6 anchovy fillets, drained and finely
    chopped (optional)
salt and ground black pepper

1 Heat 50ml/2fl oz/¹⁄₄ cup of the oil in a large frying pan. Add the bread cubes and garlic. Fry, stirring and turning constantly, until the cubes are golden brown all over. Drain on kitchen paper. Discard the garlic.

2 Tear large lettuce leaves into smaller pieces. Then put all the lettuce in a bowl. Add the remaining oil to the lettuce and season with salt and plenty of ground black pepper. Toss well to coat the leaves.

3 Break the eggs on top. Sprinkle with the lemon juice. Toss well again to combine. Add the Parmesan cheese and anchovies, if using. Toss gently to mix.

4 Scatter the fried bread cubes on top and serve immediately.

Nutritional information per portion: Energy 198kcal/824kJ; Protein 5.6g; Carbohydrate 13.8g, of which sugars 1.7g; Fat 13.8g, of which saturates 2.1g; Cholesterol 50mg; Calcium 64mg; Fibre 0.9g; Sodium 400mg.

Pear and Parmesan salad

This is a good starter when pears are at their seasonal best. Try Packhams or Comice when plentiful, drizzled with a poppy-seed dressing and topped with shavings of Parmesan.

SERVES 4

4 just-ripe dessert pears
50g/2oz piece Parmesan cheese
watercress, to garnish
water biscuits or rye bread,
to serve (optional)

FOR THE DRESSING

30ml/2 tbsp extra virgin olive oil
15ml/1 tbsp sunflower oil
30ml/2 tbsp cider vinegar or white
wine vinegar
2.5ml/¹/₂ tsp soft light brown sugar
good pinch of dried thyme
15ml/1 tbsp poppy seeds
salt and ground black pepper

1 Cut the pears in quarters and remove the cores. Cut each pear quarter in half lengthways and arrange them on four small serving plates. Peel the pears if you wish, though they look more attractive unpeeled.

2 Make the dressing. Mix the oils, vinegar, sugar, thyme and seasoning in a jug. Whisk well, then tip in the poppy seeds. Trickle the dressing over the pears. Garnish with watercress and shave Parmesan over the top. Serve with water biscuits or thinly sliced rye bread, if you like.

Nutritional information per portion: Energy 193kcal/804kJ; Protein 5.4g; Carbohydrate 15.7g, of which sugars 15.7g; Fat 12.5g, of which saturates 3.7g; Cholesterol 13mg; Calcium 167mg; Fibre 3.3g; Sodium 141mg.

Green bean and sweet red pepper salad

Serrano chillies are very fiery, so be cautious about their use. Wash your hands thoroughly after chopping them and make sure you don't touch your eyes.

SERVES 4

350g/12oz cooked green beans,
   quartered
2 red (bell) peppers, seeded and chopped
2 spring onions (scallions), chopped
1 or more drained pickled serrano chillies,
   rinsed, seeded and chopped
1 iceberg lettuce, coarsely shredded
olives, to garnish

FOR THE DRESSING

45ml/3 tbsp red wine vinegar
135ml/9 tbsp olive oil
salt and ground black pepper

1 Combine the cooked green beans, chopped peppers, chopped spring onions and chillies in a salad bowl.

2 Make the salad dressing. Pour the red wine vinegar into a bowl or jug. Add salt and ground black pepper to taste, then gradually whisk in the olive oil until well combined.

3 Pour the salad dressing over the prepared vegetables and toss lightly together to mix and coat thoroughly.

4 Line a large serving platter with the shredded iceberg lettuce leaves and arrange the salad vegetables attractively on top. Garnish with the olives and serve at once.

Nutritional Information per portion: Energy 270kcal/1117kJ; Protein 4.1g; Carbohydrate 9.4g, of which sugars 8.4g; Fat 25.8g, of which saturates 3.8g; Cholesterol 0mg; Calcium 55mg; Fibre 3.9g; Sodium 5mg.

Egg and fennel tabbouleh with nuts

Tabbouleh is a Middle Eastern salad of steamed bulgur wheat, flavoured with parsley, mint and garlic as well as fennel. Small whole eggs, such as quail or guinea fowl, would be good in this dish.

SERVES 4

250g/9oz/1¼ cups bulgur wheat
4 small eggs
1 fennel bulb
1 bunch spring onions (scallions), chopped
25g/1oz/½ cup sun-dried tomatoes, sliced
45ml/3 tbsp chopped fresh parsley

30ml/2 tbsp chopped fresh mint
75g/3oz/½ cup black olives
60ml/4 tbsp olive oil, preferably Greek or Spanish
30ml/2 tbsp garlic oil
30ml/2 tbsp lemon juice
salt and ground black pepper

1 Cover the bulgur wheat with boiling water and leave to soak for 15 minutes. Transfer to a metal sieve (strainer), place over a pan of boiling water, cover and steam for 10 minutes. Spread out on a metal tray and leave to cool while you cook the eggs and fennel.

2 Hard-boil the small eggs for 8 minutes. Cool under running water, shell and quarter, or, if using an egg slicer, slice not quite all the way through.

3 Halve and then finely slice the fennel. Boil in salted water for 6 minutes, drain and cool under running water.

4 Combine the egg quarters, fennel, spring onions, sun-dried tomatoes, parsley, mint and olives with the bulgur wheat. If you have sliced the eggs, arrange them on top of the salad. Dress the tabbouleh with olive oil, garlic oil and lemon juice. Season well and serve.

Nutritional information per portion: Energy 624kcal/2587kJ; Protein 13.4g; Carbohydrate 49.3g, of which sugars 1.5g; Fat 42.2g, of which saturates 6.6g; Cholesterol 190mg; Calcium 97mg; Fibre 1.9g; Sodium 83mg.

Potato salad with curry plant mayonnaise

Potato salad can be made well in advance and is therefore a useful dish for serving as an appetizer at a party. Its popularity means that there are very rarely any leftovers to be cleared away.

SERVES 6

1kg/2¼lb new potatoes, in skins
300ml/½ pint/1¼ cups home-made or
　　shop-bought mayonnaise
6 curry plant leaves, roughly chopped
salt and ground black pepper
mixed lettuce leaves or other salad
　　leaves, to serve

1 Place the potatoes in a pan of salted water, bring to the boil and cook for 15 minutes or until tender. Drain and place in a large bowl to cool slightly.

2 Mix the mayonnaise with the curry plant leaves and black pepper, and stir into the potatoes while they are still warm. Leave to cool completely, then serve on a bed of mixed lettuce leaves or other assorted salad leaves.

Nutritional information per portion: Energy 474kcal/1967kJ; Protein 4.1g; Carbohydrate 29.1g, of which sugars 4.2g; Fat 38.7g, of which saturates 6g; Cholesterol 38mg; Calcium 37mg; Fibre 2.4g; Sodium 246mg.

Tricolour salad

A popular salad, this dish depends for success on the quality of its ingredients. Mozzarella is the best cheese to serve uncooked, and ripe plum tomatoes are essential.

SERVES 2–3

150g/5oz mozzarella, thinly sliced
4 large plum tomatoes, sliced
1 large avocado
about 12 basil leaves or a small handful
    of flat leaf parsley leaves
45–60ml/3–4 tbsp extra virgin olive oil
ground black pepper
ciabatta and sea salt flakes, to serve

1 Arrange the sliced mozzarella cheese and tomatoes randomly on two salad plates. Crush over a few good pinches of sea salt flakes. This will help to draw out some of the juices from the plum tomatoes. Set aside in a cool place and leave to marinate for about 30 minutes.

2 Just before serving, cut the avocado in half using a sharp knife and twist the halves to separate. Lift out the stone (pit) and remove the peel.

3 Carefully slice the avocado flesh crossways into half moons, or cut it into large chunks if that is easier.

4 Place the avocado on the salad, then sprinkle with the basil or parsley. Drizzle over the olive oil, add a little more salt if needed and some black pepper.

5 Serve at room temperature, with chunks of crusty Italian ciabatta for mopping up the dressing.

Nutritional information per portion: Energy 526kcal/2180kJ; Protein 17.5g; Carbohydrate 8.3g, of which sugars 7.2g; Fat 47.1g, of which saturates 16g; Cholesterol 44mg; Calcium 344mg; Fibre 5.8g; Sodium 327mg.

Pear and Roquefort salad

The flavours of pear and Roquefort complement each other beautifully in this classic dish. Choose ripe, firm Comice or Williams pears.

SERVES 4

3 ripe pears
lemon juice, for tossing
about 175g/6oz mixed salad leaves
175g/6oz Roquefort cheese
50g/2oz/½ cup hazelnut kernels,
    toasted and chopped

FOR THE DRESSING
30ml/2 tbsp hazelnut oil
45ml/3 tbsp olive oil
15ml/1 tbsp cider vinegar
5ml/1 tsp Dijon mustard
salt and ground black pepper

1 To make the dressing, mix together the oils, vinegar and mustard in a bowl or screw-top jar. Add salt and black pepper to taste. Stir or shake well.

2 Peel, core and slice the pears and toss them in lemon juice.

3 Arrange the salad leaves on serving plates, then place the pears on top. Crumble the cheese and scatter over the salad with the hazelnuts. Spoon over the dressing and serve at once.

Nutritional information per portion: Energy 409kcal/1694kJ; Protein 11.6g; Carbohydrate 12.9g, of which sugars 12.5g; Fat 35g, of which saturates 11g; Cholesterol 33mg; Calcium 258mg; Fibre 3.7g; Sodium 539mg.

Asparagus and orange salad

This is a really attractive salad with lots of bright colours. A simple dressing of olive oil and vinegar mingles with the orange and tomato flavours, with great results.

SERVES 4

225g/8oz asparagus, trimmed and cut
   into 5cm/2in pieces
2 large oranges
2 well-flavoured ripe tomatoes, each
   cut into eight pieces
50g/2oz romaine lettuce leaves, shredded
30ml/2 tbsp extra virgin olive oil
2.5ml/1/2 tsp sherry vinegar
salt and ground black pepper

1 Cook the asparagus in boiling, salted water for 3–4 minutes, until just tender. Drain and refresh under cold water. Set aside.

2 Grate the rind from half an orange and reserve. Peel all the oranges and cut into segments, removing the membrane. Squeeze out the juice from the membrane and reserve.

3 Put the asparagus, orange segments, tomatoes and lettuce into a salad bowl. Mix together the oil and vinegar and add 15ml/1 tbsp of the reserved orange juice and 5ml/1 tsp of the rind. Season with salt and plenty of ground black pepper. Just before serving, pour the dressing over the salad and mix gently to coat.

Nutritional information per portion: Energy 102kcal/424kJ; Protein 2.9g; Carbohydrate 9.3g, of which sugars 9.2g; Fat 6.1g, of which saturates 0.9g; Cholesterol 0mg; Calcium 58mg; Fibre 2.9g; Sodium 9mg.

Avocado and smoked fish salad

Avocado and smoked fish make a good combination and, flavoured with herbs and spices, create a delectable and elegant starter. Smoked haddock or cod can also be used in this salad.

SERVES 4

15g/¹/₂oz/1 tbsp butter or margarine
¹/₂ onion, finely sliced
5ml/1 tsp mustard seeds
225g/8oz smoked mackerel, flaked
30ml/2 tbsp fresh chopped coriander (cilantro)
2 firm tomatoes, peeled and chopped
15ml/1 tbsp lemon juice

FOR THE SALAD

2 avocados
¹/₂ cucumber
15ml/1 tbsp lemon juice
2 firm tomatoes
1 green chilli
salt and ground black pepper

1 Melt the butter or margarine in a frying pan, add the onion and mustard seeds and fry for about 5 minutes until the onion is soft but not browned. Add the fish, chopped coriander, tomatoes and lemon juice and cook over a low heat for about 2–3 minutes. Remove from the heat and leave to cool.

2 To make the salad, slice the avocados and cucumber thinly. Place together in a bowl and sprinkle with the lemon juice to prevent discoloration. Slice the tomatoes and seed and finely chop the chilli.

3 Place the fish mixture in the centre of a serving plate. Arrange the avocado slices, cucumber and tomatoes decoratively around the outside of the fish. Or, spoon a quarter of the fish mixture on to each of four serving plates and divide the avocados, cucumber and tomatoes equally among them. Then sprinkle with the chopped chilli and a little salt and black pepper, and serve.

Nutritional information per portion: Energy 386kcal/1596kJ; Protein 12.8g; Carbohydrate 4.6g, of which sugars 3.1g; Fat 35.2g, of which saturates 8.6g; Cholesterol 67mg; Calcium 32mg; Fibre 3.4g; Sodium 455mg.

Salade Niçoise

Made with the freshest ingredients, this classic Provençal salad makes a simple yet unbeatable summer dish. Serve with country-style bread and chilled white wine for a substantial appetizer.

SERVES 4–6

1 tuna steak, about 175g/6oz
olive oil, for brushing
115g/4oz French (green) beans
115g/4oz mixed salad leaves
1/2 small cucumber, thinly sliced
4 ripe tomatoes, quartered
50g/2oz canned anchovies, drained and
    halved lengthways
4 hard-boiled eggs, quartered
1/2 bunch radishes, trimmed
50g/2oz/1/2 cup small black olives
salt and ground black pepper
flat leaf parsley, to garnish (optional)

FOR THE DRESSING

90ml/6 tbsp virgin olive oil
2 garlic cloves, crushed
15ml/1 tbsp white wine vinegar
salt and ground black pepper

1 Whisk together the oil, garlic and vinegar, then season to taste.

2 Preheat the grill (broiler). Brush the tuna steak with olive oil and season with salt and black pepper. Cook for 3–4 minutes on each side until seared on the outside. Set aside and leave to cool.

3 Trim and halve the French beans. Cook them in a pan of boiling water for 2 minutes until only just tender, then drain, refresh and leave to cool.

4 Mix together the salad leaves, sliced cucumber, quartered tomatoes and French beans in a large, shallow bowl. Cut the tuna steak into two pieces or more, if you prefer.

5 Arrange the tuna over the salad, with the drained anchovies, hard-boiled eggs, radishes and small black olives. Pour over the dressing and then toss together lightly. Serve garnished with flat leaf parsley, if using.

Nutritional information per portion: Energy 218kcal/903kJ; Protein 12.3g; Carbohydrate 3.4g, of which sugars 3.2g; Fat 17.4g, of which saturates 3.2g; Cholesterol 135mg; Calcium 50mg; Fibre 1.7g; Sodium 256mg.

Smoked trout pasta salad

The fennel and dill really complement the flavour of the smoked trout in this delicious dish and the little pasta shells catch the trout, creating tasty mouthfuls.

SERVES 8

15g/1/2oz/1 tbsp butter
175g/6oz/1 cup chopped fennel bulb
6 spring onions (scallions), 2 finely
   chopped and the rest thinly sliced
225g/8oz skinless smoked trout
   fillets, flaked
45ml/3 tbsp chopped fresh dill

120ml/4fl oz/1/2 cup mayonnaise
10ml/2 tsp fresh lemon juice
30ml/2 tbsp whipping cream
450g/1lb/4 cups small pasta shapes, such
   as conchiglie
salt and ground black pepper
dill sprigs, to garnish

1 Melt the butter in a small pan. Cook the fennel and minced spring onions for 3–5 minutes. Transfer to a large bowl and cool slightly.

2 Add the sliced spring onions, trout, dill, mayonnaise, lemon juice and cream. Season and mix.

3 Bring a large pan of water to the boil. Salt to taste and add the pasta. Cook according to the instructions on the packet until just al dente. Drain thoroughly and leave to cool.

4 Add the pasta to the vegetable and trout mixture and toss to coat evenly. Check seasoning and add salt and ground black pepper, if necessary. Serve the salad lightly chilled or at room temperature, garnished with sprigs of dill.

Nutritional information per portion: Energy 369kcal/1548kJ; Protein 14.5g; Carbohydrate 42.7g, of which sugars 2.8g; Fat 16.8g, of which saturates 4g; Cholesterol 29mg; Calcium 31mg; Fibre 2.3g; Sodium 613mg.

Mixed seafood salad

If you cannot find all the seafood included in this dish in fresh form, then use a combination of fresh and frozen, but do use what is in season first.

SERVES 6–8

350g/12oz small squid
1 small onion, cut into quarters
1 bay leaf
200g/7oz raw unpeeled prawns (shrimp)
675g/1¹/₂lb fresh mussels, in the shell
450g/1lb small fresh clams
175ml/6fl oz/³/₄ cup white wine
1 fennel bulb

FOR THE DRESSING

75ml/5 tbsp extra virgin olive oil
45ml/3 tbsp lemon juice
1 garlic clove, finely chopped
salt and ground black pepper

1 Working near the sink, clean the squid by first peeling off the thin skin from the body section. Rinse well. Pull the head and tentacles away from the sac section. Some of the intestines will come away with the head. Remove and discard the translucent quill and any remaining insides from the sac. Sever the tentacles from the head. Discard the head and intestines. Remove the small hard beak from the base of the tentacles. Rinse the sac and tentacles of the squid well under cold running water. Drain in a colander.

2 Bring a large pan of water to the boil. Add the onion and bay leaf. Drop in the squid and cook for about 10 minutes, or until tender. Remove with a slotted spoon, and allow to cool before slicing into rings 1cm/¹/₂in wide. Cut each tentacle section into 2 pieces. Set aside.

3 Drop the prawns into the same boiling water, and cook until they turn pink, for about 2 minutes. Remove with a slotted spoon. Peel and remove the intestinal vein. (The cooking liquid may be strained and kept to make a soup. When cool, store in the freezer if not using immediately.)

4 Cut off the "beards" from the mussels. Scrub and rinse the mussels and clams well in several changes of cold water. Place in a large pan with the wine. Cover, and steam until all the shells have opened. (Discard any that do not open.) Lift the clams and mussels out.

5 Remove all the clams from their shells with a small spoon. Place in a large serving bowl. Remove all but 8 of the mussels from their shells, and add them to the clams in the bowl. Leave the remaining mussels in their half shells, and set aside. Cut the green, ferny part of the fennel away from the bulb. Chop finely and set aside. Chop the bulb into bite-size pieces, and add it to the serving bowl with the squid and prawns.

6 Make a dressing by combining the oil, lemon juice, garlic and chopped fennel green in a small bowl. Add salt and pepper to taste. Pour over the salad, and toss well. Decorate with the remaining mussels in the half shell. This salad may be served either at room temperature or lightly chilled.

Nutritional information per portion: Energy 166kcal/693kJ; Protein 19.3g; Carbohydrate 2.9g, of which sugars 1g; Fat 8.6g, of which saturates 1.3g; Cholesterol 177mg; Calcium 65mg; Fibre 0.9g; Sodium 480mg.

Wilted spinach and bacon salad

The spinach does not need to be cooked in this salad, as the hot dressing wilts it and provides a glorious taste sensation with the crispy bacon rashers.

SERVES 6

450g/1lb fresh young spinach leaves
225g/8oz streaky (fatty) bacon rashers
25ml/1½ tbsp vegetable oil
60ml/4 tbsp red wine vinegar
60ml/4 tbsp water
20ml/4 tsp caster (superfine) sugar
5ml/1 tsp mustard powder
8 spring onions (scallions), thinly sliced
6 radishes, thinly sliced
2 hard-boiled eggs, coarsely grated
salt and ground black pepper

1 Pull any coarse stalks from the spinach leaves and rinse well. Put the leaves in a large salad bowl.

2 Fry the bacon rashers in the oil until crisp and brown. Remove with tongs and drain on kitchen paper. Reserve the cooking fat in the pan. Chop the bacon and set aside until needed.

3 Combine the vinegar, water, sugar, mustard, and salt and ground black pepper in a bowl and stir until smoothly blended. Add to the fat in the frying pan and stir to mix. Bring the dressing to the boil, stirring.

4 Pour the hot dressing evenly over the spinach leaves. Scatter the bacon, spring onions, radishes and eggs over, and toss, then serve.

Nutritional information per portion: Energy 161kcal/667kJ; Protein 10.7g; Carbohydrate 5.3g, of which sugars 5.2g; Fat 10.9g, of which saturates 3.2g; Cholesterol 83mg; Calcium 148mg; Fibre 1.9g; Sodium 708mg.

Melon and prosciutto salad

Sections of cool fragrant melon wrapped with slices of air-dried ham make a delicious salad appetizer. If strawberries are in season, serve with a savoury-sweet strawberry salsa.

SERVES 4

1 large cantaloupe, Charentais or
  Galia melon
175g/6oz prosciutto or Serrano ham,
  thinly sliced

FOR THE SALSA
225g/8oz/2 cups strawberries
5ml/1 tsp caster (superfine) sugar
30ml/2 tbsp groundnut (peanut) or
  sunflower oil
15ml/1 tbsp orange juice
2.5ml/½ tsp finely grated orange rind
2.5ml/½ tsp finely grated fresh
  root ginger
salt and ground black pepper

1 Halve the melon and scoop the seeds out with a spoon. Cut the rind away with a paring knife, then slice the melon thickly. Chill until ready to serve.

2 To make the salsa, hull the strawberries and cut them into large dice. Place in a small mixing bowl with the sugar and crush lightly to release the juices. Add the oil, orange juice, rind and ginger. Season with salt and plenty of black pepper.

3 Arrange the melon on a serving plate, lay the ham over the top and serve with a bowl of salsa, handed round separately.

Nutritional information per portion: Energy 147kcal/614kJ; Protein 9.2g; Carbohydrate 12.2g, of which sugars 12.2g; Fat 7.1g, of which saturates 1.2g; Cholesterol 25mg; Calcium 29mg; Fibre 1.1g; Sodium 568mg.

Guide to techniques

This section looks at how garnishes

can transform an appetizer into something

really special by just adding a swirl of

cream or a sprig of parsley. In addition,

there are recipes for marinades to

tenderize fish or meat, and oils and

dressings that enhance the flavour of

crisp salad vegetables.

Garnishes

Many garnishes are delicate works of art; others add a dash of texture or a hint of colour. Most garnishes are simple to do and that extra touch transforms a dish into something very special.

CREAM SWIRL

A swirl of cream or yogurt makes a bowl of soup look attractive.

1 Transfer cream to a jug (pitcher) with a good pouring lip. Pour a swirl on the surface of each bowl of soup.

2 Draw the tip of a fine skewer quickly through the cream to create a delicate feathered pattern. Serve the soup immediately.

CROÛTONS

Crispy croûtons use up stale bread and add crunch to any dish.

Cut the bread into small cubes, brush with oil and bake in the oven. Croûtons will keep in an airtight container for up to a week.

PARMESAN CURLS

Curls of Parmesan add a delicate touch to pasta or risotto.

Holding a vegetable peeler at a 45 degree angle, draw it steadily across the block of Parmesan cheese to form a curl.

CHILLI FLOWERS

Make these chilli flowers several hours before they are needed. This will allow the "flowers" to open up.

1 Cut a chilli lengthways from the tip to within 1cm/$\frac{1}{2}$in of the stem end. Repeat at intervals around the chilli.

2 Rinse the chillies in cold running water and remove all the seeds. Place the chillies in a bowl of iced water and leave to chill for at least 4 hours.

3 For very curly flowers, leave the chillies in water in a cold place overnight. Wash your hands, knife and chopping board afterwards.

LEMON TWIST

This classic garnish is simple to make, but very effective.

Cut a lemon into thin slices. Make a cut in each slice from the centre to the skin. Hold either side of the cut and twist to form an "S" shape.

CHIVE BRAIDS

Try floating a couple of edible braids of chives in a bowl of soup.

1 Hold three chives down with a bowl on one end. Plait the chives to within 2.5cm/1in of the end.

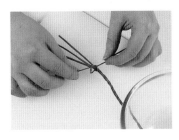

2 Tie a chive around each end of the plait. Trim both ends.

3 Pour boiling water over the braid in a bowl. Drain and refresh under cold running water. Drain again.

TOMATO SUNS

Colourful cherry tomato suns look good with most dishes, but especially with pâtés and terrines.

1 Place a tomato stem-side down. Cut lightly into the skin across the top, edging the knife down towards the base on either side. Repeat until the skin has been cut into eight separate segments, which are still joined at the base.

2 Carefully slide the top of the knife under the point of each segment and gradually ease the skin away towards the base. Gently fold the petals back to mimic the sun's rays.

AVOCADO FAN

Versatile avocados can serve as edible containers, be sliced or diced in a salad, or form the foundation of a soup or sauce. They also make very elegant garnishes.

1 Halve, stone (pit) and peel an avocado. Slice each half lengthways into quarters. Carefully and gently draw a cannelle knife (zester) across the quarters at 1cm/1/2in intervals, to create regular stripes.

2 Make four cuts lengthways down each avocado quarter leaving 1cm/1/2in intact at the end. Carefully fan out the slices and arrange on a plate as a pretty garnish.

SPRING ONION TASSELS

This garnish is very popular in Chinese restaurants, where the appearance of a dish is as important as the taste. Spring onion (scallion) tassels will embellish most Chinese meals. Choose the freshest and crispest spring onions you can find with as much white part as possible.

Using a sharp knife, cut the white part of a spring onion into a 6cm/21/2in length. Shred one end, then place the spring onion in iced water for 30 minutes until the ends curl. Make several more tassels in the same way.

Marinades, oils and **dressings**

Marinades, flavoured oils and dressings can turn a piece of fish into a delectable appetizer or hors d'oeuvre. With a few ingredients, you can make a herb marinade to tenderize meat, a ginger and garlic oil for fried dishes, or a sour cream dressing to bring out the flavour of a crisp salad.

SUMMER HERB MARINADE

Make the best of summer herbs with this marinade. Any combination may be used, depending on what you have to hand, and it works well with veal, chicken, pork or lamb.

1 Discard any coarse and broken stalks, as well as any wilted and damaged leaves, from a wide selection of herb sprigs, such as chervil, thyme, parsley, sage, chives, rosemary and oregano, then, using a sharp knife, chop finely.

2 Mix the herbs with 90ml/6 tbsp olive oil, 45ml/3 tbsp tarragon vinegar, 1 garlic clove, crushed, 2 spring onions (scallions), chopped, and seasoning in a bowl. Add the meat or poultry, cover and chill for 2–3 hours.

GINGER AND LIME MARINADE

This refreshing marinade is particularly good with chicken.

1 Mix together the rind of one lime and the juice of three limes. Add 15ml/1 tbsp green cardamom seeds, crushed, 1 finely chopped onion, grated fresh root ginger (use a 2.5cm/1in piece and peel before grating), 1 large garlic clove, crushed and 45ml/3 tbsp olive oil.

2 Pour over the meat or fish. Stir gently to coat.

3 Cover the marinating meat and leave in a cool place for 2–3 hours.

CHILLI AND GARLIC MARINADE

Add extra chillies to this delicious marinade, but only if you like your food to be very spicy.

Combine 4 small chillies, seeded and finely diced, 10ml/2 tsp finely grated fresh root ginger, 1 large garlic clove, crushed, and 45ml/3 tbsp light soy sauce in a bowl. Add the meat or fish, cover and chill for 2– 4 hours.

CHINESE MARINADE

This marinade is traditionally used to flavour succulent duck breasts.

Mix 15ml/1 tbsp clear honey, 1.5ml/1¼ tsp five-spice powder, 1 garlic clove, finely chopped, 15ml/ 1 tbsp hoisin sauce and a pinch of salt and pepper in a large shallow bowl or dish. Add the duck breasts or other meat, turning them in the marinade. Cover with cling film (plastic wrap) and leave in a cool place to marinate for 2 hours.

ABOVE: *Flavourings for aromatic oils include cinnamon, coriander, fennel, garlic, chillies and ginger.*

AROMATIC SPICE OIL

As well as tasting delicious, oils make wonderful gifts. You can use many combinations of ingredients, such as chillies, coriander and lime leaves. Peel and bruise a 6cm/2¹/₂in piece of fresh root ginger and place in a bottle. Fill with groundnut (peanut) oil, 2 garlic cloves and 3 small peeled shallots. Cover and leave in a cool dark place for 2 weeks before using.

SPICY TOMATO DRESSING

This tangy dressing goes extremely well with a robust salad, such as bean or potato salad. It can also be used as a delicious marinade for meat. Mix together 5ml/1 tsp ground cumin, 15ml/1 tbsp tomato ketchup, 30ml/2 tbsp olive oil, 15ml/1 tbsp white wine vinegar and 1 garlic clove, crushed in a small bowl. Add a little salt and some hot pepper sauce to taste and stir again thoroughly.

SOUR CREAM AND DILL DRESSING

This unusual dressing can be made in only a couple of minutes.

Blend together 120ml/4fl oz/¹/₂ cup sour cream, 10ml/2 tsp creamed horseradish and 15ml/1 tbsp chopped fresh dill in a small bowl and season with a little salt and freshly ground black pepper. Use accordingly if not using immediately, store the dressing in the refrigerator.

HERB GARDEN DRESSING

The dried mixture will keep throughout the winter until your herbs are growing again. It can also be used to sprinkle over vegetables, casseroles and stews.

1 Mix together 115g/4oz/1 cup dried oregano, 115g/4oz/1 cup dried basil, 50g/2oz/¹/₂ cup dried marjoram, 50g/2oz/¹/₂ cup dried dill, 50g/2oz/¹/₂ cup dried mint leaves, 50g/2oz/¹/₂ cup onion powder, 30ml/2 tbsp dry mustard, 10ml/2 tsp salt and 15ml/1 tbsp freshly ground black pepper and keep in a sealed jar to use as needed.

2 When making a batch of salad dressing, take 2 tbsp of the herb mixture and add it to 350ml/ 12fl oz/1¹/₂ cups of extra virgin olive oil and 120ml/4fl oz/¹/₂ cup cider vinegar in a bowl or jug (pitcher).

3 Mix the dressing thoroughly and allow to stand for 1 hour or so. Mix again before using.

Index

A

aromatic spice oil 221
artichokes
   charred artichokes with lemon oil
      dip 118
asparagus
   asparagus and egg terrine 90–1
   asparagus and orange salad 207
   asparagus with raspberry dressing
      109
   chilled asparagus soup 64
   grilled asparagus with salt-cured
      ham 46
   marinated asparagus and
      langoustine 169
aubergines
   baba ganoush with Lebanese
      flatbread 20–1
   Greek aubergine and spinach pie
      110–11
avocados
   avocado fan 219
   avocado and smoked fish salad
      208
   avocado soup 60
   gazpacho with avocado salsa 52–3
   guacamole 16
   prawn, egg and avocado mousses
      88
   tortilla wrap with tabbouleh and
      avocado 126

B

baba ganoush with Lebanese
   flatbread 20–1
baby carrot and fennel soup 62–3
bacon
   wilted spinach and bacon
      salad 204
baked Mediterranean vegetables 113
barbecue-glazed chicken skewers 178
basil and lemon dip 14–15
beans
   cannellini bean and rosemary
      bruschetta 104–5
   chilli bean dip 24–5

clams with chilli and yellow bean
   sauce 164–5
green bean and sweet red pepper
   salad 201
lemon, thyme and bean stuffed
   mushrooms 103
beansprouts
   soya beansprout soup 58
beef
   beef satay with a hot mango
      dip 29
   spicy koftas 185
bread
   baba ganoush with Lebanese
      flatbread 20–1
   breaded sole batons 137
   broccoli soup with garlic toast 75
   cannellini bean and rosemary
      bruschetta 104–5
   chive scrambled eggs in brioche
      122
   croûtons 218
   griddled tomatoes on soda bread
      100
   prawn toasts 47
broccoli soup with garlic toast 75
brochettes see skewers
buckwheat blinis with mushroom
   caviar 132

C

caesar salad 199
cannellini bean and rosemary
   bruschetta 104–5
capers
   marinated feta cheese with capers
      114–15
carrots
   baby carrot and fennel soup 62–3
celeriac fritters with mustard
   dip 13
charred artichokes with lemon oil
   dip 118
cheese
   cheese aigrettes 36
   crab and ricotta tartlets 151
   fried rice balls stuffed with
      mozzarella 129
   goat's cheese salad 196–7
   golden Parmesan chicken 174
   marinated feta cheese with capers
      114–15
   mini baked potatoes with blue
      cheese 127
   Parmesan curls 218
   Parmesan fish goujons 27
   Parmesan thins 37
   pear and Parmesan salad 200
   pear and Roquefort salad 206
   pear and Stilton 133

twice-baked Gruyère and potato
   soufflé 128
wild mushroom and fontina
   tarts 120–1
chicken
   barbecue-glazed chicken skewers
      178
   chicken bitki 180
   chicken with lemon and
      garlic 175
   chicken liver pâté 81
   chicken parcels 179
   chicken and pork terrine 96–7
   chicken satay with peanut sauce
      32–3
   golden Parmesan chicken 174
   tandoori chicken sticks 176–7
chickpeas
   hummus bi tahina 10–11
   sesame seed-coated falafel with
      tahini dip 117
chilled soups see soups
chilli
   chilli bean dip 24–5
   chilli flowers 218
   chilli and garlic marinade 220
   clams with chilli and yellow bean
      sauce 164–5
   courgette fritters with chilli jam
      116
Chinese marinade 220
chives
   chive braids 219
   chive scrambled eggs in brioche
      122
chorizo pastry puffs 45
clams
   clams with chilli and yellow bean
      sauce 164–5
   mussels and clams with lemon
      grass 162
coconut
   lemon and coconut dhal dip 18–19
courgette fritters with chilli jam 116
crabs
   crab cakes with tartare sauce
      160–1
   crab and ricotta tartlets 151
   hot crab soufflés 158–9
cream
   cream swirl 218
   soured cream and dill dressing 221
crispy spring rolls 40–1
croûtons 218
cucumber
   chilled prawn and cucumber
      soup 54
   cucumber flowers 218
   Thai fish cakes with cucumber
      relish 144–5

tzatziki 22
curried parsnip soup 69

D

deep-fried dishes
   deep-fried lamb patties 184
   deep-fried new potatoes with
      saffron aioli 108
   deep-fried whitebait 139
dips
   baba ganoush with Lebanese
      flatbread 20–1
   basil and lemon dip 14–15
   beef satay with a hot mango
      dip 29
   celeriac fritters with mustard dip
      13
   charred artichokes with lemon oil
      dip 118
   chilli bean dip 24–5
   guacamole 16
   hummus bi tahina 10–11
   king prawns in crispy batter 26
   king prawns with spicy dip 28
   lemon and coconut dhal dip 18–19
   potato skewers with mustard dip
      107
   potato skins with Cajun dip 12
   quail's eggs with herbs and dips 23
   sesame seed-coated falafel with
      tahini dip 117
   Thai tempeh cakes with dipping
      sauce 17
   tzatziki 22
dolmades 102
dressings
   asparagus with raspberry dressing
      109
   herb garden dressing 221
   soured cream and dill dressing 221
   spicy tomato dressing 221
duck wontons with spicy mango
   sauce 34–5

E

eggs
   asparagus and egg terrine 90–1
   chive scrambled eggs in brioche
      122
   egg and fennel tabbouleh with
      nuts 202–203
   eggs benedict 193
   eggy Thai fish cakes 43
   hot crab soufflés 158–9
   pickled quail's eggs 39
   poached eggs Florentine 101
   prawn, egg and avocado
      mousses 88
   quail's eggs in aspic with
      prosciutto 192
   quail's eggs with herbs and dips 22–3

risotto frittata 119
son-in-law eggs 112
tapenade and quail's eggs 42
twice-baked Gruyère and potato
   soufflé 128

F
fennel
   baby carrot and fennel soup 62–3
   egg and fennel tabbouleh with
      nuts 202–3
fish
   avocado and smoked fish salad
      208
   breaded sole batons 137
   deep-fried whitebait 139
   eggy Thai fish cakes 43
   fish sausages 138
   haddock and smoked salmon
      terrine 94–5
   herby plaice fritters 140
   mixed seafood salad 212–13
   monkfish packages 142
   Parmesan fish goujons 27
   potted salmon with lemon and
      dill 86
   salmon cakes with butter
      sauce 143
   salmon rillettes 84–5
   salmon and scallop brochettes 168
   seafood pancakes 152–3
   sea trout mousse 82–3
   smoked haddock pâté 78
   smoked salmon pâté 79
   smoked trout pasta salad 210-11
   Thai fish cakes with cucumber
      relish 144–5
   Thai-style seafood turnovers
      148–9
   three-colour fish kebabs 136
five-spice rib-sticker 48
French onion and morel soup 71
fresh tomato soup 65
fried rice balls stuffed with
   mozzarella 129
fritters
   celeriac fritters with mustard
      dip 13
   courgette fritters with chilli
      jam 116
   herby plaice fritters 140
   vegetable tempura 123

G
garlic
   broccoli soup with garlic
      toast 75
   chicken with lemon and garlic 175
   chilli and garlic marinade 220
   deep-fried new potatoes with
      saffron aioli 108
   garlic prawns in filo tartlets 170–1
   Spanish garlic soup 56–7
   gremolata 218–19
gazpacho with avocado salsa 52–3
ginger and lime marinade 220

Glamorgan sausages 106
goat's cheese salad 196–7
golden Parmesan chicken 174
Greek aubergine and spinach pie
   110–11
green bean and sweet red pepper
   salad 201
griddled tomatoes on soda bread 100
grilled asparagus with salt-cured
   ham 46
grilled vegetable terrine 92–3
guacamole 16

H
haddock see fish
ham
   grilled asparagus with salt-cured
      ham 46
   melon and prosciutto salad 215
   quail's eggs in aspic with Parma
      ham 192
herbs
   basil and lemon dip 14–15
   cannellini bean and rosemary
      bruschetta 104–5
   chive braids 219
   chive scrambled eggs in
      brioches 122
   herb garden dressing 221
   herbed liver pâté pie 80
   herby plaice fritters 140
   lemon, thyme and bean stuffed
      mushrooms 103
   mussels and clams with lemon
      grass 162
   pork balls with a minted peanut
      sauce 30
   potted salmon with lemon and
      dill 86
   quail's eggs with herbs and dips 22–3
   scallop-stuffed roast peppers with
      pesto 163
   soured cream and dill dressing 221
   summer herb marinade 220
hot crab soufflés 158–9
hot-and-sour soup 55
hummus bi tahina 10–11

I
Italian prawn skewers 156

K
kebabs see skewers

L
lamb
   deep-fried lamb patties 184
   lamb tikka 182–3
   skewered lamb with red onion
      salsa 49
   spicy koftas 185
langoustine
   marinated asparagus and
      langoustine 169
leek and onion tartlets 124–5
lemons

basil and lemon dip 14–15
charred artichokes with lemon oil
   dip 118
chicken with lemon and garlic 175
lemon and coconut dhal 18–19
lemon, thyme and bean stuffed
   mushrooms 103
lemon twist 219
potted salmon with lemon and dill
   86
liver
   chicken liver pâté 81
   herbed liver pâté pie 80

M
Malayan prawn laksa 66–7
mangos
   beef satay with a hot mango
      dip 29
   duck wontons with spicy mango
      sauce 34–5
marinades
   beef satay with a hot mango dip 29
   chicken satay with peanut sauce
      32–33
   chilli and garlic marinade 220
   Chinese marinade 220
   ginger and lime marinade 220
   lamb tikka 182–3
   marinated asparagus and
      langoustine 169
   marinated feta cheese with capers
      114–15
   marinated mussels 146–7
   summer herb marinade 220
   tandoori chicken sticks 176–7
melon and prosciutto salad 215
mini baked potatoes with blue
   cheese 127
mixed seafood salad 212–13
monkfish packages 142
mousses
   prawn, egg and avocado mousses
      88
   sea trout mousse 82–3
mushrooms
   buckwheat blinis with mushroom
      caviar 132
   French onion and morel soup 71
   lemon, thyme and bean stuffed
      mushrooms 103

tortellini chanterelle broth 68
wild mushroom and fontina
   tarts 120–1
wild mushroom soup 72–3
mussels
   marinated mussels 146–7
   mussels and clams with lemon
      grass 162
   scallop and mussel kebabs 166–7

N
nuts
   chicken satay with peanut sauce
      32–3
   egg and fennel tabbouleh with
      nuts 202–3
   pork balls with a minted peanut
      sauce 30
   pork and peanut wontons with
      plum sauce 31
   spicy peanut balls 38

O
onions
   French onion and morel soup 71
   leek and onion tartlets 124–5
   skewered lamb with red onion
      salsa 49
   spring onion tassels 219
oranges
   asparagus and orange salad 207

P
paella croquettes 141
panzanella salad 198
Parmesan see cheese
parsnips
   curried parsnip soup 69
pasta
   smoked trout pasta salad 210–11
   tortellini chanterelle broth 68
   vermicelli soup 61
pâté
   chicken liver pâté 81
   herbed liver pâté pie 80
   smoked haddock pâté 78
   smoked salmon pâté 79
peanuts see nuts
pears
   pear and Parmesan salad 200
   pear and Roquefort salad 206
   pear and Stilton 133
peas
   split pea soup 70
peppers
   chilled tomato and sweet pepper
      soup 76–7
   green bean and sweet red pepper
      salad 201
   roast pepper terrine 88–89
   scallop-stuffed roast peppers with
      pesto 163
pies
   Greek aubergine and spinach pie
      110–11
   herbed liver pâté pie 80

savoury pork pies 188–9
plaice *see* fish
poached eggs Florentine 101
pork
  chicken and pork terrine 96–7
  five-spice rib-sticker 48
  pork balls with a minted peanut
    sauce 30
  pork and peanut wontons with
    plum sauce 31
  pork satay 186–7
  savoury pork pies 188–9
potatoes
  deep-fried new potatoes with
    saffron aioli 108
  mini baked potatoes with blue
    cheese 127
  potato salad with curry plant
    mayonnaise 204
  potato skewers with mustard dip
    107
  potato skins with Cajun dip 12
  twice-baked Gruyère and potato
    soufflé 128
potted prawns 87
potted salmon with lemon and dill 86
prawns
  aromatic tiger prawns 154–5
  chilled prawn and cucumber
    soup 54
  garlic prawns in filo tartlets 170–1
  Italian prawn skewers 156
  king prawns in crispy batter 26
  king prawns with spicy dip 28
  Malayan prawn laksa 66–7
  potted prawns 87
  prawn cocktail 157
  prawn, egg and avocado mousses
    88
  prawn toasts 47

Q
quail's eggs *see* eggs

R
raspberries
  asparagus with raspberry
    dressing 109
rice
  fried rice balls stuffed with
    mozzarella 129
  paella croquettes 141
  risotto alla Milanese 181

risotto frittata 119
spinach and rice soup 74
roast pepper terrine 88–89

S
salads
  asparagus and orange salad 207
  avocado and smoked fish salad
    208
  caesar salad 199
  goat's cheese salad 196–7
  green bean and sweet red pepper
    salad 201
  melon and prosciutto salad 215
  mixed seafood salad 212–13
  panzanella salad 198
  pear and Parmesan salad 200
  pear and Roquefort salad 206
  potato salad with curry plant
    mayonnaise 204
  salade Niçoise 209
  smoked trout pasta salad 210–11
  tricolour salad 205
  wilted spinach and bacon
    salad 204
salmon *see* fish
salsa
  gazpacho with avocado salsa 52–3
  skewered lamb with red onion
    salsa 49
samosas 44
satay
  beef satay with a hot mango
    dip 29
  chicken satay with peanut sauce
    32–3
  pork satay 186–7
sausages
  chorizo pastry puffs 45
  fish sausages 138
  Glamorgan sausages 106
  mini sausage rolls 190–1
savoury pork pies 188–9
scallops
  salmon and scallop brochettes 168
  scallop and mussel kebabs 166–7
  scallop-stuffed roast peppers with
    pesto 163
sea trout mousse 82–3
seafood *see* fish
sesame seed-coated falafel with
  tahini dip 117
skewers
  barbecue-glazed chicken skewers
    178
  Italian prawn skewers 156
  potato skewers with mustard
    dip 107
  salmon and scallop brochettes 168
  scallop and mussel kebabs 166–7
  skewered lamb with red onion
    salsa 49
  tandoori chicken sticks 176–7
  three-colour fish kebabs 136
smoked trout pasta salad 210–11
sole *see* fish

son-in-law eggs 112
soups
  avocado soup 60
  baby carrot and fennel soup 62–3
  broccoli soup with garlic toast 75
  chilled asparagus soup 64
  chilled prawn and cucumber
    soup 54
  chilled tomato and sweet pepper
    soup 76–7
  curried parsnip soup 69
  French onion and morel soup 71
  fresh tomato soup 65
  gazpacho with avocado
    salsa 52–3
  hot-and-sour soup 55
  Malayan prawn laksa 66–7
  soya beansprout soup 58
  Spanish garlic soup 56–7
  spinach and tofu soup 59
  spinach and rice soup 74
  split pea soup 70
  tortellini chanterelle broth 68
  vermicelli soup 61
  wild mushroom soup 72–3
soured cream and dill dressing 221
Spanish garlic soup 56–7
spices
  aromatic spice oil 221
  curried parsnip soup 69
  deep-fried new potatoes with
    saffron aioli 108
  duck wontons with spicy mango
    sauce 34–5
  five-spice rib-sticker 48
  king prawns with spicy dip 30
  mussels and clams with lemon
    grass 162
  spicy koftas 185
  spicy peanut balls 38
  spicy tomato dressing 221
  tandoori chicken sticks 176–7
  turkey, juniper and peppercorn
    terrine 95
spinach
  Greek aubergine and spinach pie
    110–11
  poached eggs Florentine 101
  spinach and tofu soup 59
  spinach empanadillas 150
  spinach and rice soup 74
  wilted spinach and bacon
    salad 214
split pea soup 70
spring onion tassels 219
spring rolls 44

T
tabbouleh
  egg and fennel tabbouleh with
    nuts 202–3
  tortilla wrap with tabbouleh and
    avocado 126
tahini
  hummus bi tahina 10–11
  sesame seed-coated falafel with

tahini dip 117
tandoori chicken sticks 176–7
tapenade and quail's eggs 42
tarts
  crab and ricotta tartlets 151
  garlic prawns in filo tartlets 170–1
  leek and onion tartlets 124–5
  vegetable tarte tatin 130–1
  wild mushroom and fontina
    tarts 120–1
terrines
  asparagus and egg terrine 90–1
  chicken and pork terrine 96–7
  grilled vegetable terrine 92–3
  haddock and smoked salmon
    terrine 94–5
  roast pepper terrine 88–89
  turkey, juniper and peppercorn
    terrine 95
Thai dishes
  eggy Thai fish cakes 43
  Thai fish cakes with cucumber
    relish 144–5
  Thai tempeh cakes with dipping
    sauce 17
  Thai-style seafood turnovers
    148–9
three-colour fish kebabs 136
tofu
  spinach and tofu soup 59
tomatoes
  chilled tomato and sweet pepper
    soup 76–7
  fresh tomato soup 65
  griddled tomatoes on soda
    bread 100
  spicy tomato dressing 221
  tomato suns 219
  tortellini chanterelle broth 68
tortilla wrap with tabbouleh and
  avocado 126
tricolour salad 205
trout *see* fish
turkey, juniper and peppercorn
  terrine 95
twice-baked Gruyère and potato
  soufflé 128
tzatziki 22

V
vegetables
  baked Mediterranean vegetables
    113
  grilled vegetable terrine 92–3
  vegetable tarte tatin 130–1
  vegetable tempura 123
vermicelli soup 61

W
watercress
whitebait *see* fish
wilted spinach and bacon
  salad 214
wontons
  duck wontons with spicy mango
    sauce 34–5